Outline of Stratificational Grammar

by

Sydney M. Lamb

With an Appendix by

Leonard E. Newell

Georgetown University Press
Washington, D.C. 20007

Printed in the United States of America
Library of Congress Catalog Card Number 66-28562

Preface

The first edition of the *Outline of Stratificational Grammar* was hastily written and multilithed in 1962 for sale to students at the A.S.U.C. Bookstore in Berkeley and for distribution as a report of the Machine Translation Project of the University of California. It was intended as an interim document, to serve temporarily in lieu of a fuller treatment of stratificational theory which was then being planned and is still in preparation. In 1964, when copies of that Outline were no longer available, I was persuaded by Robert Lado and C.I.J.M. Stuart of the School of Languages and Linguistics, Georgetown University, to provide a new edition for wider distribution. I have delayed in doing so until now mainly because my time has been occupied with other writing on various aspects of stratificational theory.

This new version of the Outline is also a rather hasty interim document, but it is at least more up to date, less compact, and generally less shoddy than the original one. The revision has been extensive, and there have been several additions. In the first Outline the emphasis was on linguistic description, and the treatment of properties of linguistic structure was subordinate to that aim and was scattered and very sketchy. This version has been reorganized, and the characterization of linguistic structure has been emphasized, expanded, and consolidated (Chapter II). Of the other changes, some are of course the results of discoveries of various properties of linguistic structure that have been made since 1962; others are merely changes of terminology and notation. I now make extensive use of graphic notation, and I have attached much less importance to algebraic notation than in the first Outline. The pursuit of simplicity in linguistic description was treated separately for the realizational portion of a stratal system and the tactics in the first Outline, whereas a unified more general treatment is given here (in Chapter III).

In my work on many of the points treated in the Outline I have been aided by various colleagues and by my students, who have contributed ideas and have smoothed the rough edges of mine; I am particularly grateful to H. A. Gleason, Jr., M. A. K. Halliday, Peter A. Reich, Leonard E. Newell, and David L. Bennett. Mr. Bennett has also assisted by drawing the diagrams. Exercises 1, 4, and 12 are modified versions of problems originally devised by William F. Shipley and included in the first Outline; also repeated here are the Natchez problem of Mary R. Haas (Exercise 6) and a Latin problem of Murray B. Emeneau (Exercise 5). The index was prepared by Amy Shaughnessy.

Sydney M. Lamb

New Haven, Connecticut
31 May 1966

CONTENTS

I. INTRODUCTION

Ardhamātrālāghavena putrotsvam manyante vaiyākaraṇāḥ
"Grammarians rejoice more over the saving of half a mora than over the birth of a son."

Paribhāṣā 122

The system presented here is called stratificational because one of its chief features is its treatment of linguistic structure as comprising several structural layers or strata. A language, by its nature, relates sounds (or graphs, i.e. marks on paper or the like) to meanings; the relationship turns out to be a very complex one, which can be analyzed in terms of a series of code-like systems each of which has a structure analogous to that which some earlier linguistic theories ascribed to language as a whole. For example, each of these systems has its own syntax or tactics, so that a linguistic structure as a whole has a series of tactic components rather than just one. These several systems may be called STRATAL SYSTEMS, and each may be said to be associated with a STRATUM of linguistic structure.

The question of how many stratal systems there are in a linguistic structure as a whole can be answered only by empirical investigation, and it remains to be determined whether or not all natural languages have the same number of strata. Evidence available so far suggests that all natural languages have at least four, and that at least some languages, including English, have six strata. A six-stratum structure may be regarded as made up of three major components, SEMOLOGY, GRAMMAR, and PHONOLOGY, each of which comprises two stratal systems. Such a three-way division into major components is perhaps appropriate for all natural languages, but until further research is done it remains an open question whether each of the three major components in every language comprises exactly two stratal systems. Some of the discussion in this outline has specific reference to the six-stratum scheme; thus it remains undetermined whether such discussion applies to all languages or only to a typological subset of all languages, namely the class of languages which have six strata.

Of the three major components, semology is related to meaning and phonology to speech, while grammar is intermediate between the two. The term GRAMMAR is used in three different senses in this Outline, and it is hoped that the contexts will be sufficiently different that no confusion will result: first, to refer to this middle component of a linguistic structure; second, to refer to a structural description of all or part of a grammar in the first sense; third (the sense of the term in the title "Outline of Stratificational Grammar"), with reference to the general considerations involved in writing structural descriptions of linguistic systems, i.e. considerations which apply for semology and phonology as well as for grammar in the narrower sense.

One of the reasons for the complexity of linguistic structure, i.e. for the fact that it comprises several stratal systems rather than just one or two, is that sounds and meanings are, by their natures, patterned separately from each other; they each have their own structural relationships. Phonological systems must be adapted to the articulatory and auditory organs, while semological systems must be adapted to thought patterns and to the phenomena, events, and relationships about which people think and talk. Moreover, phonological systems must conform to the fact that speech takes place in time, which is linear; but no such restriction is imposed upon semological systems, and on the contrary, the things to which semological systems must relate — events, phenomena, experiences, relationships, and the like — are often multidimensional. Thus a close correspondence between semological and phonological systems would be impossible. The same situation exists for written languages because writing systems are generally based upon spoken languages, so that they tend to have close correspondence to phonological systems but not to semologies. This situation may be contrasted with that of notational systems which have been developed independently of spoken languages and which have taken advantage of the two-dimensional character of paper and blackboards to allow for closer correspondence to meaning than would be possible for one-dimensional expression systems. Examples are the notational systems used for diagrams of organic compounds in chemistry, electronic circuit diagrams, and flow diagrams for computer programs. (It is this same consideration which underlies the desirability of a two-dimensional diagramming notation, such as that used in this Outline, for linguistic structure.)

Another factor is that a language has the property of allowing its speakers to speak of anything in the range of their experience and imagination while employing only a very small number of different fundamental phonological elements. Thus the number of elements at the lowest stratum of a language is only around fifteen, while the elements at the highest stratum number well into the thousands.

The concept of stratification in language is by no means original with me, nor are many other features of this system, which is no more than the result of adding a few extensions and refinements to a synthesis of Hjelmslev's glossematics (1943) and one of the standard versions of American structural linguistics.[1] The present formulation differs from earlier ones mainly in recognizing more strata and in that it provides a more precise specification of the relationships on which the concept of stratification is based. It derives partly from the work of Hockett (e.g. 1947c, 1954, 1958), but differs from it by recognizing more strata. That earlier, "proto-stratificational," framework had just two strata, phonemic and morphemic, which were approximately at the levels of the hypophonemes and the lexons, respectively, of the system presented here.

Linguistic Analysis

A language may be regarded as a system of relationships. As such, it is not directly observable. The linguist can only observe the manifestations of linguistic structure, i.e. samples of speech and/or writing, and the situations in which they occur. From analyzing such data he must try to construct a representation of the system of relationships which underlies it. Such a representation may be taken as a description of (part of) the language. Thus the goal of a linguistic description should be a characterization, as precise as possible, of the structural relationships which underlie the linguistic data. This is not the same as describing the manifestations of the linguistic structure directly, nor does it mean simply providing a list of rewrite rules for deriving manifestations of linguistic structure from other manifestations of linguistic structure.

Linguistic analysis can perhaps best be understood as a process of simplifying. It is a process in which the analyst finds recurrences of similar entities having such relationships among themselves and with other entities that they can be regarded, at some level, as repetitions of one another. Once found, such recurrent entities may be extracted and described only once instead of repeatedly. This process amounts to a simplification, and it also involves generalization. The phenomena dealt with are then better understood and are better treated in whatever applications may be desired.

Except for the various refinements which are necessary, there is little more to linguistic analysis, reduced to its essentials, than making observations similar to those of the student in ninth-grade algebra to the effect that, e.g.

$$abc + abd + abe + abf + abg$$

may be reduced to

$$ab\ (c + d + e + f + g).$$

The latter expression is simpler than the former and it contains a generalization not present in the former. It is simpler precisely by virtue of the fact that it expresses the generalization. The fact of the occurrence of *ab* in five separate combinations has been stated once instead of five separate times. What the algebra student does when he factors the first expression is not essentially different from what the linguist does when he determines that

blueberry, cranberry

can be reduced to

blue
cran] berry

(Note that just as the algebra student doesn't have to ask whether or not *c, d, e, f,* or *g* occur in any other combinations before he performs his factoring operation, so also the linguist segments *cranberry* because *berry* occurs in other combinations, even if *cran* doesn't.)

The old Hindu saying quoted above actually expresses what is perhaps the most important and powerful single principle of linguistic analysis. Another important principle is that linguistic analysis should be based on such criteria that any (competent) independent investigator applying them to the same material would arrive at an equivalent solution. A third is that a language should be described in its own terms, and not by the application of an external mold. This last principle also applies to areas within linguistic structure. Thus, for example, the pattern of arrangement of morphemes should be described in its own terms, not by the application of phonological criteria. Similarly, it is both reprehensible and unnecessary to attempt to define units of the tactics of phonemes, such as syllables, by the use of phonetic entities, such as chest pulses. In other words, a good procedure of tactic analysis is one which allows the patterns of arrangement to reveal themselves, while that analysis is bad which applies to a system, from the outside, a predetermined structure.

It is convenient to distinguish two general types of linguistic analysis, concerned with two kinds of linguistic patterning. They may be called TACTIC ANALYSIS and REALIZATIONAL ANALYSIS.

Tactic Analysis

Let us consider further the algebraic example given above. The second expression, i.e.

$$ab\,(c + d + e + f + g)$$

is simpler than the first. The simpler version shows the result of finding a recurrent partial similarity and isolating it. The same type of process lies at the basis of tactic analysis. A simple illustration is provided by the following forms:

big boy	big man	big dog	big cat
sad boy	sad man	sad dog	sad cat
wet boy	wet man	wet dog	wet cat

One way to describe the fact of the occurrence of these forms in English is that just used: one may list the forms. Fór this description it was necessary to make 24 item-identifications. Another way to account for the same data is as follows:

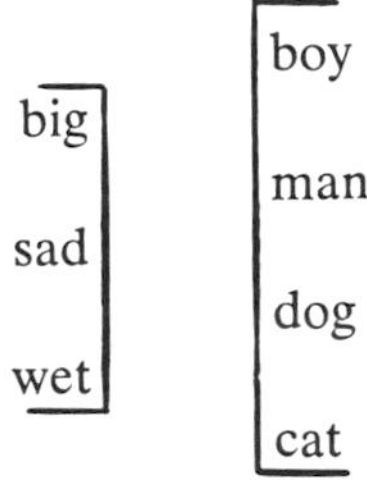

or simply (*big, sad, wet*) (*boy, man, dog, cat*). The latter description requires only seven item-identifications. The excess surface information of the first description is seventeen item-identifications, i.e. 24 minus 7; and if one cares to count, one will see that those 17 excess identifications are entirely accounted for as repetitions in the first description. When one is dealing with classes of hundreds of items, the difference is of course more striking. Moreover, the former approach to description is not even theoretically possible in general, since the number of combinations generated by a tactic system as a whole is infinite.

Simple as it appears, this process of isolating recurrent partial similarities is the basis of tactic analysis. If the traditional equipment of tactic analysis is reduced to its essentials, it turns out to involve little more than applying a simple factoring operation like that performed by the ninth-grade algebra student. This process leads the analyst to distribution classes and constructions which describe arrangements in the simplest possible terms. Questions concerning immediate constituency are automatically answered; and the criteria which have been put forth for determination of immediate constituents (cf. Wells 1947, Nida 1949: Chap. 4), insofar as they are valid at all, are derivable from a more basic simplicity principle.

Realizational Analysis

Analysis concerned with the parts of a stratal system other than its tactics may be called REALIZATIONAL ANALYSIS. Such analysis involves four basic types of operations: HORIZONTAL GROUPING, HORIZONTAL SPLITTING, VERTICAL SPLITTING, and VERTICAL GROUPING. An example of HORIZONTAL GROUPING is the recognition that elements *c, a, t* combine, in that order, to form a structural unit *cat* to be identified in such forms as *cats, catlike, catgut,* etc., but not in *cattle* or *caterpillar.* HORIZONTAL SPLITTING is illustrated by the analysis of French *au* as a realization of the underlying combination *à le.* VERTICAL SPLITTING involves distinguishing two or more higher level units (e.g. the past participle lexon and the past tense lexon of English) realized by the same lower level unit (e.g. *-ed*). Note that *au* is a realization of the combination *à le,* i.e. of *à* AND *le,* whereas any occurrence of *-ed* is a realization of either the past participle lexon OR the past tense lexon. VERTICAL GROUPING involves the recognition that two or more units (e.g. *-ed, -en*) are alternate realizations of a single higher level unit (the past participle lexon). In practice, none of these four operations can be performed in isolation, nor is there any sequence in which they must be performed; rather, they are generally carried out together, with reference to one another.

These operations are motivated by the simplicity principle and by the need to account for the linguistic data. Failure to carry one of them out, where the possibility is available, would mean either that the description would be failing to account for certain data or that it would be stating certain relationships repeatedly which might be stated only once. For example, failure to distinguish past participles from past tense forms in English would entail a failure to accurately distinguish between grammatical and ungrammatical sentences; but the failure to recognize in *-ed* a neutralized realization of the past participle lexon and the past tense lexon would entail the repetition of various morphological and phonological relationships which apply to *-ed* without regard to which of the two lexons is represented. The failure to perform a vertical grouping operation with respect to *good* and *bett-* (of *better*) would entail repetition of various semological properties; failure to recognize French *au* as a realization of the combination *à le* would complicate the morphotactic description of French as well as that of higher levels.

It is customary, and perhaps easiest, for linguistic analysis to start at or near the bottom of linguistic structure (i.e. in the phonology) and to work upwards. In the past it has often been thought that linguistic analysis *must* proceed in a series of orderly steps from the bottom upwards, and that it must follow a prescribed procedure; but demands of this type are too severe and are unnecessary. There is no necessity of doing a complete analysis at one level before going on to the next. If the analyst desires to attempt only a very rough analysis of one level before starting to work on the next higher one, and then to revise his preliminary analysis on the basis of what he learns from his examination of the higher stratum, he should feel free to do so. The structure of a language is an integrated whole with close interrelationships among neighboring subsystems, and therefore one can hardly be sure about the correctness of his solution for one subsystem of the language until the analysis of neighboring subsystems has been done. Thus the analyst must be allowed to revise his solution in one area after working on a higher level. And why should one want to prevent him from doing so? Those not familiar with the history of linguistics during the forties and fifties may well wonder why. But it happens that there was a widely held view that a linguistic description should not be considered valid unless it could be shown that it was arrived at or could have been arrived at by the application of a mechanical step-by-step procedure. As a result, much linguistic theory of the forties and fifties consisted of attempts to devise such mechanical procedures (none of which were successful). The motivation for such stringency was that it provided a means of satisfying the important requirement that linguistic analysis be based on such principles that any (competent) independent investigator applying them to the same data would arrive at an equivalent solution. What was overlooked by most linguists during this period was that there is another far simpler way of meeting this requirement. It is to have the criteria for linguistic description stated simply as specifications which a linguistic description must meet.

Criteria of this type are to be used for testing proposed descriptions rather than for prescribing procedures of analysis. Such criteria specify the properties of an acceptable solution. With this approach, the analyst has much greater freedom. He can jump around from one level of analysis to another at will. He can use meaning whenever he wants to (notwithstanding earlier teachings to the contrary). He may also use intuition, hunches, and trial-and-error techniques. But when he arrives at a description, he must subject it to the test. In actual practice, he will be keeping the testing criteria in mind all along as he conducts his analysis, performing it so that the requirements will be satisfied. This approach does not in any way deny the value of various valuable analytical tools and techniques which a linguist should know; but these belong to the practical side of linguistics rather than to linguistic theory.

Note to Chapter One

1 Actually, the three-way primary division of linguistic structure, and with it the terms *phonology, morphology, semology, phoneme, morpheme,* and *sememe,* were used over fifty years ago by the Swedish linguist Noreen (1903-18).

II. LINGUISTIC STRUCTURE

. . . *a totality does not consist of things but of relationships* . . .

Louis Hjelmslev

I consider a language to be a system of relationships. It may be analyzed into a series of subsystems, called STRATAL SYSTEMS, each of which has a syntax or tactics and certain other characteristic patterns of relationships. The elementary relationships of which these patterns are composed are of a very small number of types.

In analyzing and describing linguistic relationships it is a matter of practical necessity to employ some system of precise and simple notation. Some linguists have been saddened by the increasing use of algebraic notation in linguistics and have longed for the "good old days" in which linguistic descriptions were written in ordinary words. Unfortunately, in those good old days linguistic descriptions were neither very complete nor very precise. Languages are such complicated systems that none but the most gifted mentalities, if even they, can cope with their structural intricacies unless aided by notational devices. To engage in linguistic description without the use of a notational system well suited to the purpose makes no more sense than to try to do long division with Roman numerals. It has sometimes been objected that if linguistic descriptions are written in a special notation rather than in ordinary words they are no longer accessible to the untutored general public. But it is better to have precise descriptions, even if they can be read only after training, than not to have precise descriptions at all. One wonders how far physics and chemistry would have progressed if similar objections had dissuaded them from using notational devices.

A two-dimensional graphic notation appears to be superior to algebraic notation for some types of work with linguistic structure, while for other purposes algebraic notation is more convenient. It is therefore desirable to employ notational systems of both types, designed so that they are mechanically interconvertible (as is done in electronics). The diagrammatic notation used here provides a more direct portrayal of structural relationships than the algebraic, and it may be considered the primary notation, while the algebraic notation may be regarded as a means of describing structural diagrams, and thus only indirectly a means of describing linguistic structures. In addition, it is convenient to employ a tabular notation for some descriptive purposes, as illustrated by Newell in the Appendix to this Outline.

LINGUISTIC GRAPHS are made up of LINES and NODES, i.e. places where lines intersect. Three fundamental dichotomies provide eight types of nodes, of which at least seven play a very important role in characterizing

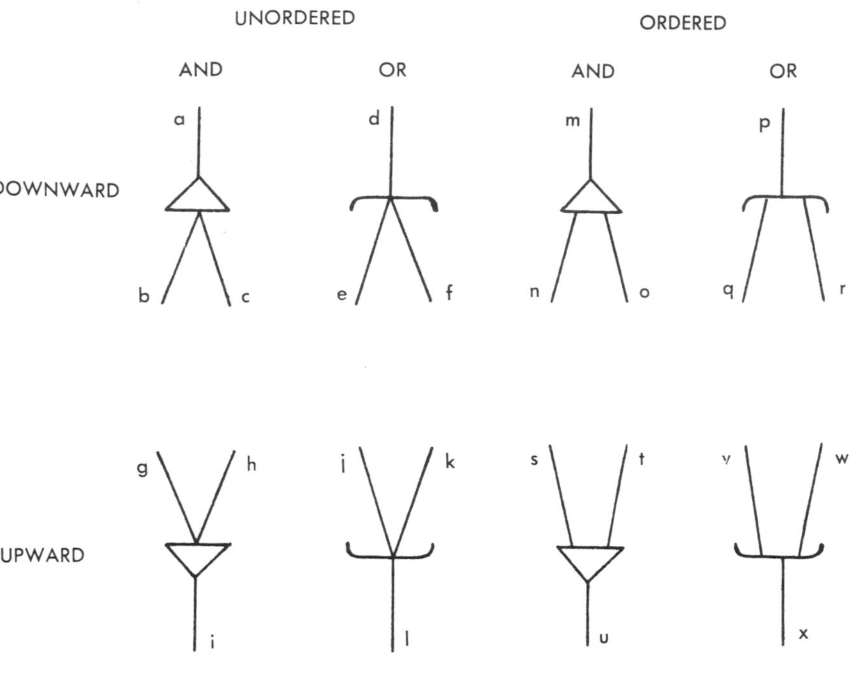

Figure 1.

linguistic structures. These dichotomies are AND:OR, UPWARD:DOWNWARD, ORDERED:UNORDERED. The eight types of nodes are shown in relation to these dichotomies in Figure 1, and the corresponding algebraic notation is as follows:

Unordered Downward And	a / b·c
Unordered Downward Or	d / e,f
Unordered Upward And	g·h / i
Unordered Upward Or	j,k / l
Ordered Downward And	m / n o
Ordered Downward Or	p / q + r
Ordered Upward And	s t / u
Ordered Upward Or	v + w / x

The directions UPWARD and DOWNWARD are in keeping with the diagramming convention according to which meaning is at the "top" and speech at the "bottom" of linguistic structure. Thus UPWARD means "towards meaning" while DOWNWARD means "towards expression." Note that in the algebraic notation the diagonal clearly indicates the direction since it has an upper side (at left) and a lower side (at right). Where convenient, the diagonal of opposite direction may be used. Thus

$$x \setminus y \cdot z$$

means the same as

$$y \cdot z \,/\, x$$

The OR is an exclusive OR; and the ordering with respect to the AND relationship is temporal ordering, while ordering with respect to an OR is an ordering of priority; i.e., that which comes first takes priority over the second if both are possible. These relationships are perhaps most easily understood in terms of the dynamic interpretation which can be given to linguistic diagrams, which enables them to serve as models of the processes involved in producing and decoding speech. For the dynamic interpretation, IMPULSES are allowed to move along the lines, in either direction. Impulses move downward during the production process and upward during the decoding process. Let ^{D}a stand for "an impulse moving downward along line a" or, for short, "down a"; and let ^{U}a stand for "an impulse moving upward along line a" or "up a". Then the dynamic interpretation of the relationships listed above and diagrammed in Figure 1 is as follows (the locution "results in" may be used instead of "goes to" if one prefers):

$a \,/\, b \cdot c$	^{D}a goes to ^{D}b AND ^{D}c (simultaneously) ^{U}b AND ^{U}c (together) go to ^{U}a
$d \,/\, e, f$	^{D}d goes to ^{D}e OR ^{D}f ^{U}e OR ^{U}f goes to ^{U}d
$g \cdot h \,/\, i$	^{D}g AND ^{D}h (together) go to ^{D}i ^{U}i goes to ^{U}g AND ^{U}h (simultaneously)
$j, k \,/\, l$	^{D}j OR ^{D}k goes to ^{D}l ^{U}l goes to ^{U}j OR ^{U}k
$m \,/\, n\ o$	^{D}m goes to ^{D}n AND then (afterwards) to ^{D}o ^{U}n AND, after it, ^{U}o go to ^{U}m
$p \,/\, q + r$	^{D}p goes to ^{D}q if possible, OR else to ^{D}r ^{U}q OR ^{U}r goes to ^{U}p
$s\ t \,/\, u$	^{D}s AND, after it, ^{D}t go to ^{D}u ^{U}u goes to ^{U}s AND then (afterwards) to ^{U}t
$v + w \,/\, x$	^{D}v OR ^{D}w goes to ^{D}x ^{U}x goes to ^{U}v if possible, OR else to ^{U}w

Note that the impulse moves upward from a downward ordered AND (e.g. up *m*) only after the second (or last) impulse from below (e.g. up *o*) has reached the element; the preceding impulse(s) from below (e.g. *n*) wait at the element until the last impulse from below arrives there.

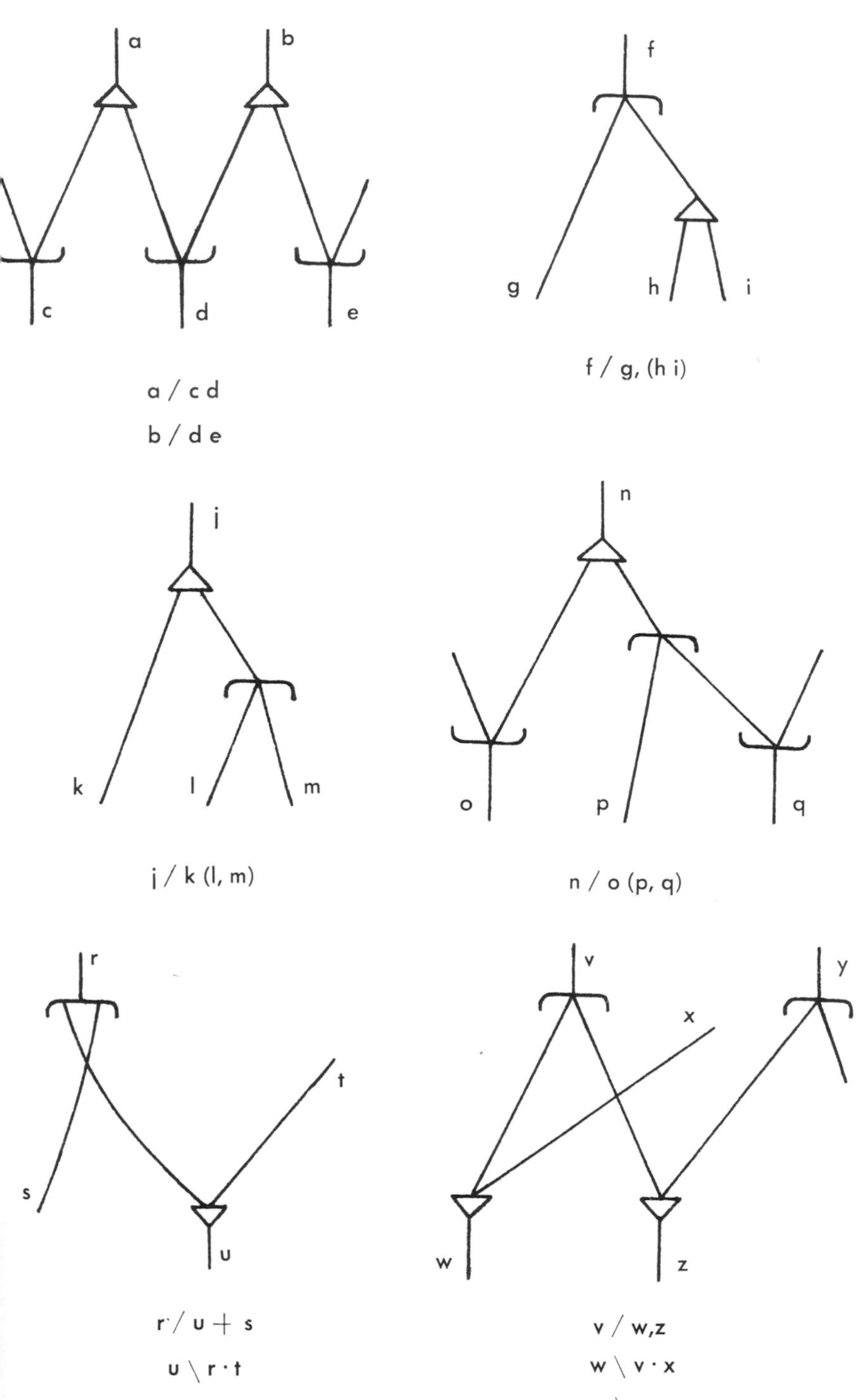
a
b
c
d
e
a / c d
b / d e
f
g
h
i
f / g, (h i)
j
k
l
m
j / k (l, m)
n
o
p
q
n / o (p, q)
r
s
t
u
r / u + s
u \ r · t
v
x
y
w
z
v / w,z
w \ v · x
z \ v · y

Figure 2.

Similarly, an impulse coming down to the first connection of an upward ordered AND waits until the other connections are activated, and an impulse proceeds downward after an impulse has arrived at the second (or last) connection.

For describing linguistic graphs algebraically one may adopt the practice of using symbols (consisting of letters or combinations of letters) either for lines or for nodes. In Figure 1 the symbols (*a, b, c, . . .*) may be regarded as standing for lines; if the other alternative is adopted, they would be taken as designating the nodes to which these lines connect. Thus (with reference to Figure 1) *a* would designate the node (not shown) to which the line leading upward from the AND node connects. This AND node itself would then have some other symbol (not shown). For purposes of this Outline, the general practice adopted is to use symbols for lines. It is unnecessary, however, to use a separate symbol for each line. Some conventions whereby shortcuts can be taken in the algebraic notation are illustrated in Figure 2 with some typical configurations.

Patterns

The elementary relationships occur in a small number of recurrent types of PATTERNS. These may be called the SIGN PATTERN, the TACTIC PATTERN, the ALTERNATION PATTERN, and the KNOT PATTERN.

The SIGN PATTERN is illustrated in Figure 3, which shows parts of some sign patterns of English, namely (from upper to lower) the lexemic sign pattern, the morphemic sign pattern, and the phonemic sign pattern. Note that the AND nodes shown in the phonemic sign pattern are unordered, indicating that the (downward) components are simultaneous, whereas the ANDS are ordered in the morphemic and lexemic sign patterns. The labels of the lines shown at the bottom of the phonemic sign pattern stand for *Closed, Labial, Apical, Spirantal,* and *Nasal,* respectively. In addition to what is shown in the figure, a sign pattern can have (above the portions shown) upward ANDS and downward ORS. An example from the morphemic sign pattern of French is *au,* which has the upward components *à le,* as shown in Figure 4. This type of situation may be called PORTMANTEAU REALIZATION, while the opposite situation illustrated in Figure 3 may be called COMPOSITE REALIZATION. Note that in Figure 4, the downward ORS are shown as ordered, signifying that the line at left takes priority over that at right. In the phonemic and morphemic systems of most languages there is relatively little portmanteau realization, but it is very important in sememic systems. Examples of portmanteau realization at the sememic level are furnished by kinship terminologies (cf. Hammel et al, 1965) and such sets as: *doe, buck, fawn, venison; cow, bull, calf, beef.*

The form of the TACTIC PATTERN is illustrated by Figure 5, which describes the phonotactics of Monachi, a Utoaztecan language of California.

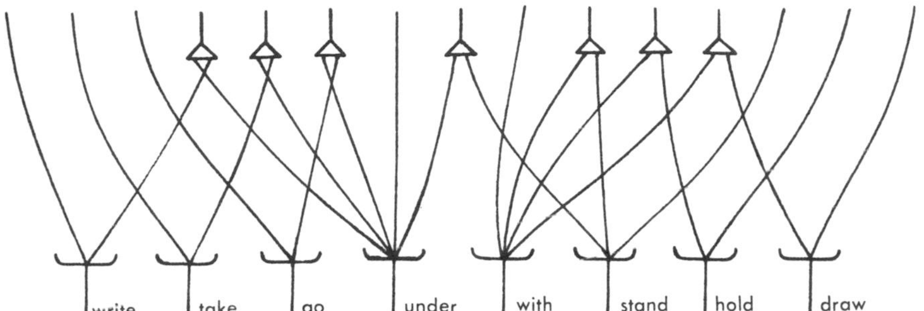

LEXEMIC

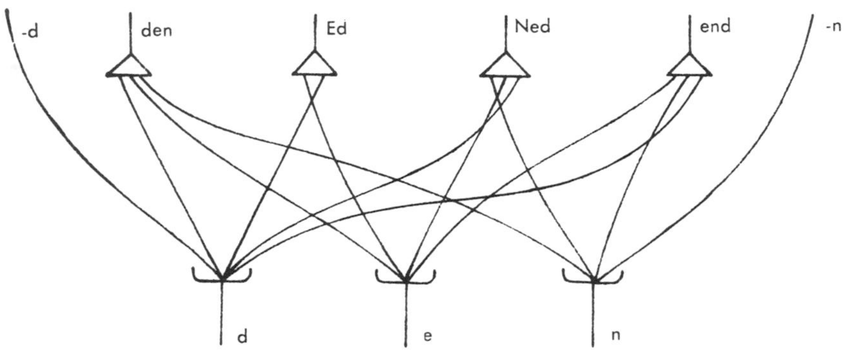

MORPHEMIC

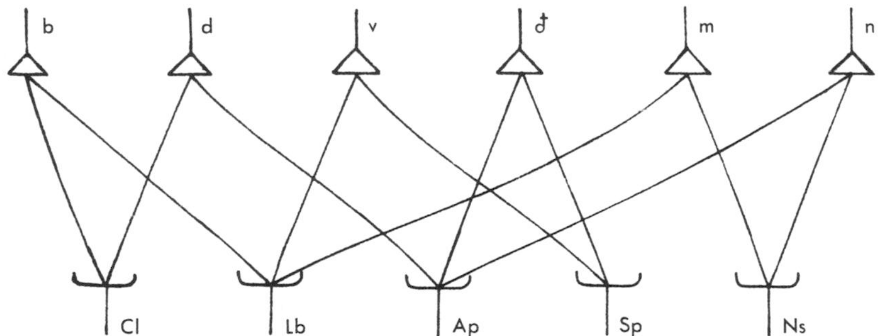

PHONEMIC

Figure 3. Sign Patterns.

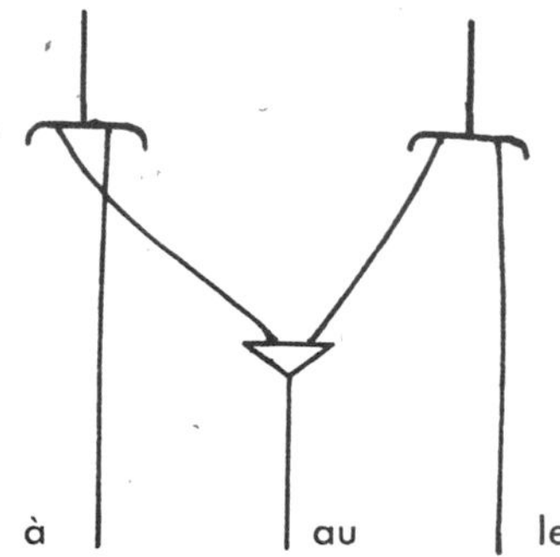

Figure 4. Portmanteau Realization in French.

(See Figure 10, page 24, and the Appendix for additional examples of tactic configurations.)

Figure 5 introduces the ZERO element, represented by a small circle at the end of a line. It is found in tactic patterns, alternation patterns, and sign patterns. Impulses moving to a zero element disappear; and an impulse may move from a zero element to the connecting line at any time. In the algebraic notation, the zero element is represented as Ø; x / y,Ø may be written x / [y] and x,Ø / y may be written [x] / y, where x and y are any symbols representing lines.

As Figure 5 illustrates, tactic patterns are in general made up largely of downward ANDS and upward and downward unordered ORS. Upward ORS in tactic patterns represent situations in which units have two or more alternative tactic functions. For example, Figure 5 shows that a glottal stop in Monachi may function either as the initial consonant or as coda of a syllable. Figure 10 below has an upward OR for nominals indicating that a nominal in English lexotactics may function as a predicate nominative, as object of a verb, as subject of a clause, or in construction with *'s* (e.g. *Mary's*). Downward ANDS in tactic patterns are often called CONSTRUCTIONS. Semotactic patterns differ from tactic patterns for lower strata in having considerable numbers of upward ANDS; occasional upward ANDS are also found in lexotactic patterns.

A tactic pattern has at its top only the zero element. The connections to the next higher stratum are not through the top of the tactics, but through the alternation pattern (see below). Thus the syllable, a phonotactic unit, does not connect upwards to anything in the morphemic system; and the morphological word, a morphotactic unit, does not lead up to anything in the lexemic system. At the bottom of the tactic pattern of a given stratal system are connections to the "emes" of that system.

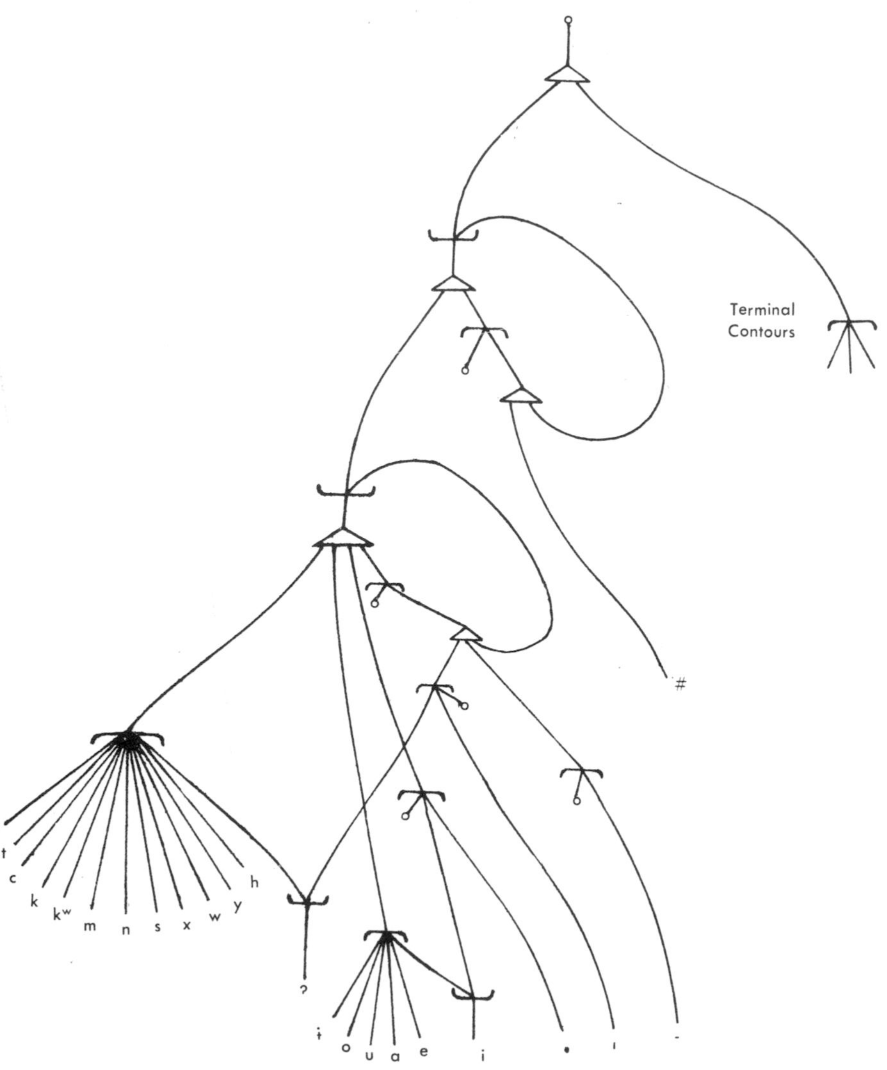

Figure 5. Monachi Phonotactics.

An ALTERNATION PATTERN has downward ORS at its top, upward ORS at its bottom. In addition there are typically relatively many lines which pass through without meeting any nodes. Part of a hypothetical alternation pattern having typical properties is shown in Figure 6, together with fragments of the other patterns present in a morphemic system. As the figure shows, the alternation pattern, sign pattern, and tactic pattern are "tied" together, as it were, by the KNOT PATTERN, which is named in accordance with this function. A knot pattern has a row of upward ANDS, which are the

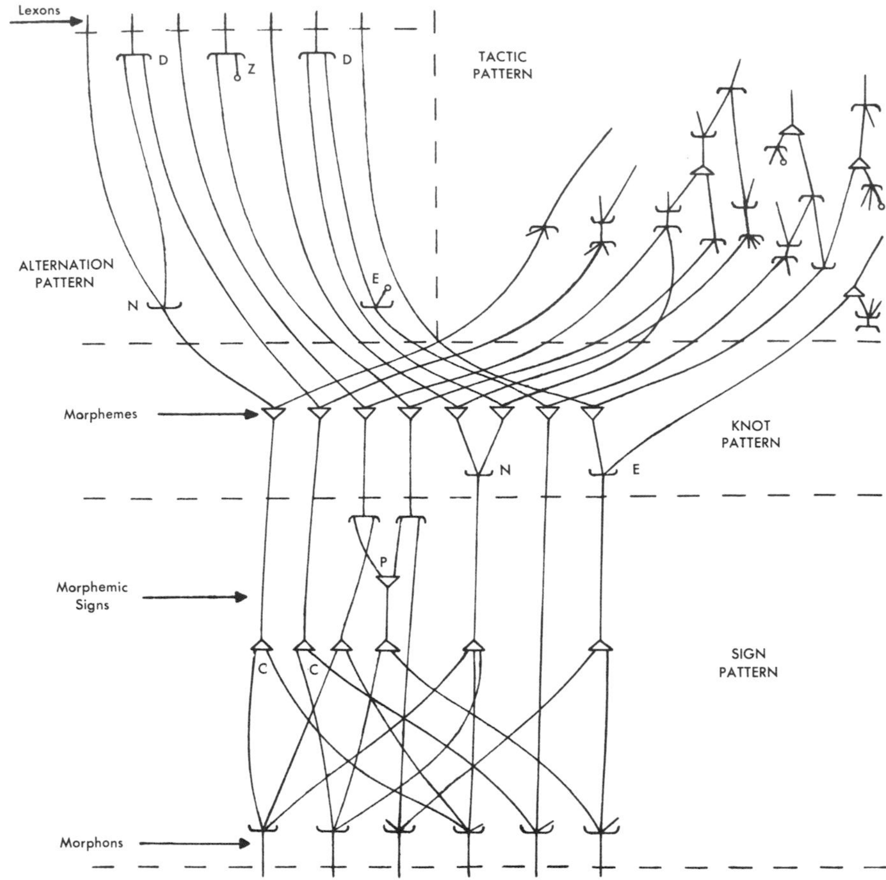

Figure 6. Part of a Morphemic System.

knots, and, below them, occasional upward ORS. The upward ANDS of the knot pattern are the "emes" of the stratal system. Thus an "eme" has a function in the tactics, a connection to the next higher stratum through the alternation pattern, and a connection to the next lower stratum through the sign pattern. In addition, a knot pattern commonly has one or more lines going upward directly to the tactic pattern rather than to upward ANDS. Such lines represent nondistinctive units, whose occurrence is determined by the tactics and which have no connection to the next higher stratum.

Figure 6 also specifies the meanings of the terms MORPHON, MORPHEMIC SIGN, MORPHEME, and LEXON. As a characterization of actual morphemic systems it is deficient in that it shows only eight morphemes, i.e. only a fragmentary sample of the hundreds of morphemes actually present in morphemic systems. (Linguistic graphs are, of course, too cumbersome to describe large quantities of relationships, and this consideration is the

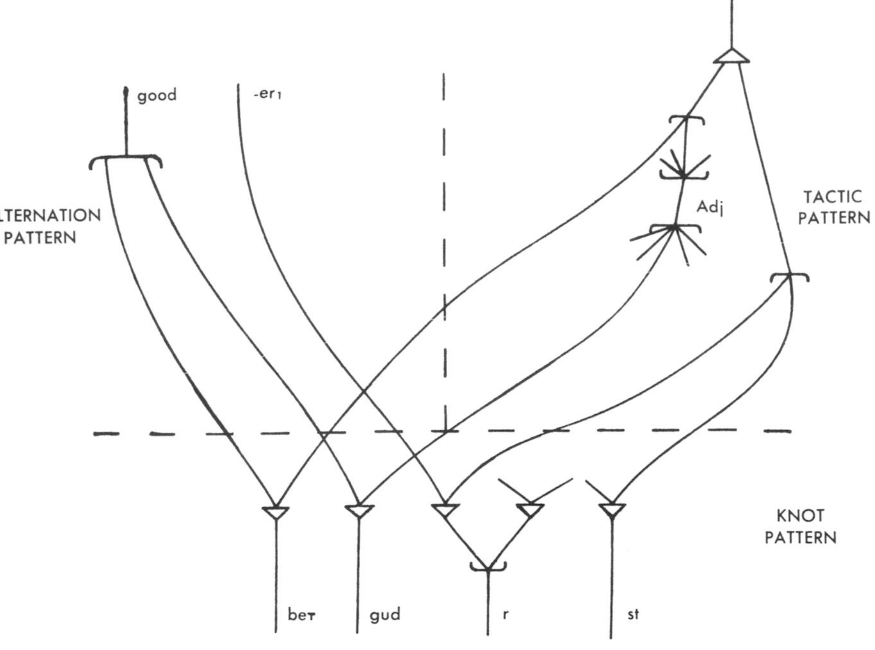

Figure 7. Morphemic Alternation in English.

primary reason for the use of an algebraic notation and a tabular notation in addition to the diagrams.)

The alternation pattern, knot pattern, and sign pattern, taken together, may be said to constitute the REALIZATIONAL PORTION of the stratal system. Any node in the realizational portion represents a discrepancy from a simple one-to-one relationship between units of neighboring strata. Terms for types of interstratal discrepancy are indicated in Figure 6 by capital letter abbreviations, whose meanings are as follows (cf. Lamb, 1964b): D, DIVERSIFICATION; Z, ZERO REALIZATION; N, NEUTRALIZATION; E, EMPTY REALIZATION; P, PORTMANTEAU REALIZATION; C, COMPOSITE REALIZATION.

Of the operations of realizational analysis mentioned above (Introduction), horizontal grouping involves recognizing instances of composite realization, while horizontal splitting is concerned with portmanteau realization. Vertical splitting is the discovery of instances of neutralization (including those involving empty realization) and the determination in each case of just where the associated upward OR is to be placed for maximum simplicity of the description; and vertical grouping is associated with diversification (including the special type called zero realization).

Figure 7 provides an illustration of diversification in the alternation pattern of the English morphemic system, together with a closely associated portion of the morphotactics. The tactic construction shown is that for the forms consisting of an adjective followed by the comparative suffix or the superlative suffix. The morpheme ^{M}/beT/ is shown as occurring only in this construction, while ^{M}/gud/ is shown as an ordinary adjective, entering into a class (cf. the downward OR) which has a variety of morphotactic functions (cf. the upward OR). (The morphon ^{MN}/T/ of ^{M}/beT/ is a special *"t"* which is realized as zero (i.e. has no phonemic realization) in *best.*) When the lexon ^{LN}/good/ occurs with ^{LN}/-er$_1$/, the tactics would allow either *better* or *gooder*, but the downward OR for ^{LM}/good/ is ordered and therefore ^{M}/beT/ takes precedence. When neither ^{LN}/-er$_1$/ nor ^{LN}/-est/ is present, the realization ^{M}/beT/ cannot occur, since the impulse from ^{LN}/good/ to ^{M}/beT/ cannot get past the upward AND unless the other line leading into it also has a downward impulse. An alternative analysis of the tactic pattern would specify that ^{M}/gud/ cannot occur in the comparative construction; but this analysis would require an unnecessarily complicated graph, since the occurrence of ^{M}/gud/ in this construction is ruled out by the ordering in the downward OR. Moreover, the analysis shown accounts for the English speaker's ability to recognize *gooder* when it is said by a child who has not yet learned this diversification (whereas, on the other hand, **betness* would not be understood as meaning the same as *goodness,* and this form is not allowed by the morphotactics).

Figure 7 also shows an example of neutralization in a knot pattern, involving the comparative *-er*$_1$ and the agentive *-er*$_2$ (as in *swimmer*). Note that, as the diagram indicates, these homophonous morphemes differ both in their meanings and in their morphotactic functions. Also present in typical knot patterns is a type of neutralization in which one line leads from the upward OR directly into the tactic pattern. Such cases have particularly attracted the attention of linguists in hypophonemic systems, and the terms NON-DISTINCTIVE FEATURE and DETERMINED FEATURE have often been used in this connection (cf. Lamb 1966b).

Strata and Terms

A STRATAL SYSTEM consists of a knot pattern, the alternation pattern and tactic pattern above it, and the sign pattern below it; except that the hypophonemic system of a language apparently lacks a sign pattern. For at least some languages it is necessary to recognize six stratal systems. In order from lowest to highest, they may be called the HYPOPHONEMIC, the (basic) PHONEMIC (cf. Lamb 1966b), the MORPHEMIC, the LEXEMIC, the SEMEMIC, and the HYPERSEMEMIC. (As an alternative, the hypophonemic and hypersememic strata might be called the PHONETIC and SEMANTIC, respectively; in this case the eme of the phonetic stratum would be the PHONETEME and that of the semantic stratum would be the SEMANTEME.)

The hypophonemic system appears not to have a sign pattern; in its place, i.e. below the hypophonemic knot pattern, is perhaps to be identified the boundary between linguistic structure and structure of another type, i.e. of a type not efficiently analyzable in terms of relationships and patterns of the type described above. Here one may speak of the MANIFESTATION of hypophonemic units (cf. Lamb 1966b). Similarly, the upper boundary of linguistic structure may be defined as the level beyond which relationships are no longer of the type described above. The question of the exact placement of this boundary and that of what type of structure lies beyond it provide important opportunities for future investigation.

The terms for linguistic units and subsystems follow a pattern which is consistent from one stratal system to another. Let X stand for any of the following: HYPOPHON(E), PHON(E), MORPH, LEX, SEM(E), HYPERSEM(E); and let X_1 precede X_2 with respect to the order of the stratal systems from lowest to highest. Then the following statements define terms for the various stratal systems: The XEMIC SYSTEM consists of the XEMIC SIGN PATTERN (except that there is perhaps no hypophonemic sign pattern), the XEMIC KNOT PATTERN, the XEMIC TACTIC PATTERN, and the XEMIC ALTERNATION PATTERN. The Xemic tactic pattern may be called the XOTACTICS; the X_1emic alternation pattern may alternately be called the X_2ONIC ALTERNATION PATTERN. Each of the upward ANDS in the Xemic knot pattern is an XEME. Each of the lines at the middle of the Xemic sign pattern (i.e. between the upward ANDS and downward ANDS) is an XEMIC SIGN. Each of the lines (or, equivalently, each of the upward ORS) at the bottom of the Xemic sign pattern is an XON. Thus an X_2on is at the bottom of the X_2emic system and at the top of the X_1emic system (specifically, at the top of its alternation pattern). The alternation pattern, knot pattern, and sign pattern of the Xemic system may be called the REALIZATIONAL PORTION of that system. The XEMIC STRATUM consists of the Xemes and the Xotactics.

The description of the realizational portion of the Xemic system may be called the XEMIC DICTIONARY or the XICON (e.g. LEXICON, MORPHICON). A description of the Xemic system may be called the XEMICS; also, the activity of analyzing the Xemic system may be called XEMICS. The Xotactic pattern, a description of the Xotactic pattern, or the activity of analyzing the Xotactic pattern may be called (triguously) XOTACTICS.

It is valuable to define a few additional units which are not in general to be found as single units anywhere within a linguistic structure but which are often important in linguistic analysis. An X_2 (e.g. MORPH) is a combination of X_1emes (e.g. phonemes) to which a downward impulse from an X_2eme (e.g. morpheme) can lead; it may also be called the X_1EMIC REALIZATION of the X_2eme; if an X_2eme has more than one X_2 (i.e. X_1emic realization), they may be called its ALLOX_2S (e.g. ALLOMORPHS).

An overall view of the relationship of various units is provided by Figure 8. In it the solid lines, and the terms connected by solid lines, represent relationships directly present in a linguistic structure. The vertical lines represent alternation patterns and the lines slanting upward to the right represent the relationships present in sign patterns plus the upward ORS of knot patterns.

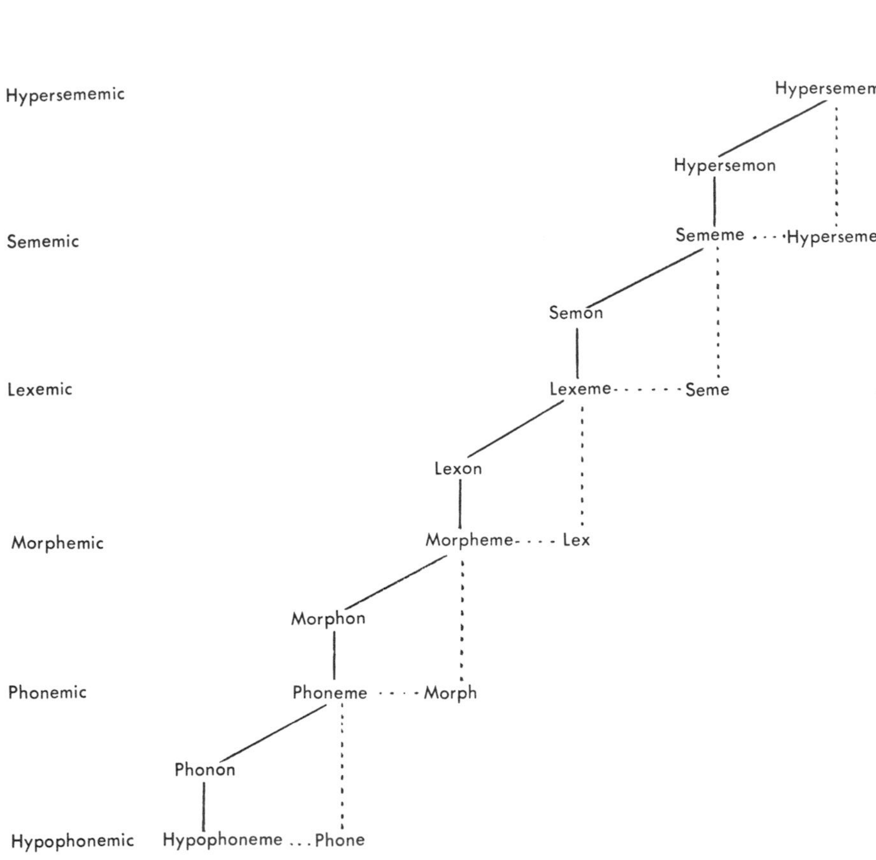

Figure 8. Some Units of Spoken Languages.

The phonemic and hypophonemic systems may be grouped together under the heading PHONOLOGY; the morphemic and lexemic systems may be grouped together under the heading GRAMMAR; and the sememic and hypersememic systems may be grouped together under the heading SEMOLOGY. Each of these terms ending in -ology may be used in three different meanings: (1) as a designation for a pair of stratal systems, i.e. a component of a linguistic structure; (2) a description of that component of a language; (3) the activity of analyzing that component.

Differences Between Strata

A stratum differs from its neighbors with regard to its elements and their combinations. The elements of a stratum, i.e. the upward ANDS of its knot pattern, are obviously unique to that stratum. Between them and the emes of a neighboring stratum there is a sign pattern and an alternation pattern, in addition to neutralization in the knot pattern. Perhaps the interstratal discrepancies occasioned by the sign patterns are the most apparent (cf. Figure 3 above), since these are obvious differences in size: between phonological components, phonological segments, morphemes, lexemes, semological components. In fact this difference has been so obvious relative to the other discrepancies that the latter have often been overlooked; linguists have often supposed that some of these different elements merely represented different tactic levels within a single tactic pattern, i.e. different RANKS (cf. Halliday 1961). Thus the division between morphology and syntax was based upon a distinction of rank by those who held it: morpology dealt with combinations of morphemes up to the rank of the word, while syntax was supposed to deal with combinations of words. The commonly held opposing view was that such a distinction was unnecessary and should not be maintained; rather, it was held, there should be a single morphotactics dealing with combinations of morphemes all the way to the rank of the sentence. Both views were incorrect, since both were attempting to deal with the tactic phenomena of grammar in terms of a single stratum. The units dealt with in syntax, properly treated, are lexemes, not words or morphemes, and they differ from morphemes in their arrangements as well as by virtue of an intervening sign pattern and an alternation pattern. Morphotactics is a tactics of morphemes, whereas syntax — i.e. lexotactics — is a tactics of lexemes. (To confuse words with lexemes, as has been quite commonly done, is to make the same mistake as that involved in confusing syllables with morphemes; the word is a tactic unit of the stratum below the lexemic, which is often but by no means always the realization of a lexeme.)

Every node in the realizational portion of a stratal system represents a difference between two strata. That is, every AND in a sign pattern involves a difference in size of units of neighboring strata; every downward OR represents an alternation among two or more units of the lower stratum realizing a single unit of the upper; every upward OR represents a neutralization of units distinct on the next higher stratum.

Less apparent at first glance is the type of difference represented by the upward ANDS of a knot pattern, since these nodes each have a single line going to the next higher stratum and a single line leading to the next lower one. But the third line, leading to the tactic pattern, represents an important interstratal discrepancy, since that tactic pattern differs from those of neighboring strata. Thus it is not in general the case that the emes of a stratum and their realizations on the next lower one occur in the same arrangements. For example, sememic arrangements generally and lexemic arrangements in part are non-linear, while combinations of morphemes appear to be generally linear (at least in many languages). The phenomenon of difference in the ordering of units (i.e. difference in the sequencing of impulses) from one level to another may be called ANATAXIS. For a simple example of a difference between lexemic and morphemic ordering, compare L/-z have-en be-en take/ with M/have -z # be -en # take -en/ (the word boundaries are provided by the morphotactics).

Differences between the ordering of morphons and that of (basic) phonemes have often been observed, and have commonly been referred to by the term *metathesis*. As an example, consider the following forms of Zoque (from Nida 1949: 67-68, 171-174), written phonemically at the left and morphonically (with morpheme boundaries indicated) at the right:

kenu	looked	ken u
kenpa	he looks, will look	ken pa
kyenhayu	he saw it for him	y ken hay u
kyenhapya	he sees it for him	y ken hay pa
kenṭoˀyu	he wanted to look	ken ṭoˀy u
kenṭoˀpya	he wants to look	ken ṭoˀy pa

This anataxis is to be accounted for as a discrepancy between the ordering of morphons, as determined by the morphotactics and the morphemic sign pattern, and the ordering which the phonotactics imposes upon (basic) phonemes. Zoque phonotactics evidently permits the sequences P/py/, P/ky/, etc. but not P/yp/, P/yk/, etc. Figure 9 shows the relevant part of the structure. Note that the upward AND for P/y/ is ordered; an impulse coming to it from the morphon MN/y/ is potentially delayed until an impulse comes from the phonotactics. Similarly, the anataxis in English between lexonic LN/-z hav -en be -ing take/ and morphemic M/have -z # be -en # take -ing/ is to be accounted for as a difference between what the morphotactics specifies and what comes to it from the lexemic system.

Two general types of anataxis may be distinguished. That illustrated above, which involves conflict between the specifications of neighboring stratal systems, may be called INTERSTRATAL ANATAXIS. The other type is directly specified within a tactic pattern and may be called INTRASTRATAL ANATAXIS. Note that in interstratal anataxis the lower tactic pattern always takes precedence over what is specified from above in encoding. In each case, the arrangement occurring on the lower stratum is that which is in

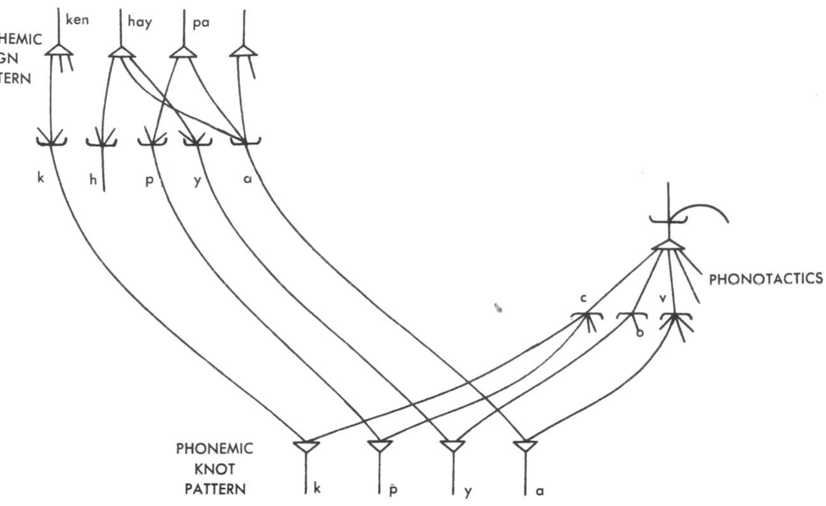

Figure 9. Morphophonemic Anataxis in Zoque.

accord with the lower tactics, despite what the higher stratal system specifies. In the case of *has been taking,* the lexemic units ᴸ/have-en/, ᴸ/be-ing/ are single lexemes, hence elementary units of the lexotactics. The lexemic sign pattern specifies that each has two components; but the lexonic ordering ᴸᴺ/-z have -en be -ing take/ is unacceptable to the morphotactics, which allows verbal suffixes to occur only after verb stems; in general, the ordering specified to a tactics from above is of importance to that tactics only for specifying the succession of choices at individual choice-points (i.e. downward ORS); but when a lexonic ordering is of elements belonging to different morphotactic classes, e.g. verb stem and verb suffix, it is up to the morphotactics to determine their relative order. Thus ᴹ/-z/ is the first verbal suffix to be selected, while ᴹ/-en/ is the second; and ᴹ/have/ is the first verb stem, while ᴹ/be/ is the second. So the morphotactics puts out, under specification of this combination of lexons, ᴹ/have -z # be -en/.

Intrastratal anataxis, on the other hand, is that which involves a difference in ordering from one level to another of a single tactic pattern. Two examples are shown in Figure 10, a simplified tentative description of a fragment of English lexotactics. In the lower right hand portion, which concerns the verb phrase (*VP*), the line leading down to the object (*Obj*) of a verb from the verb-object (*VO*) construction encounters an ordered upward AND. An impulse coming down this line to this AND will be delayed if the line labeled *d* (which is optionally active if *Av* occurs) is activated, since it is not possible for an impulse to proceed below the AND node until the impulse from line *d* reaches it. Thus the graph generates such pairs as ᴸ/take away the cat/ and ᴸ/take the cat away/, whose difference is due to whether or not the optional line *d* is taken. The other example shown in

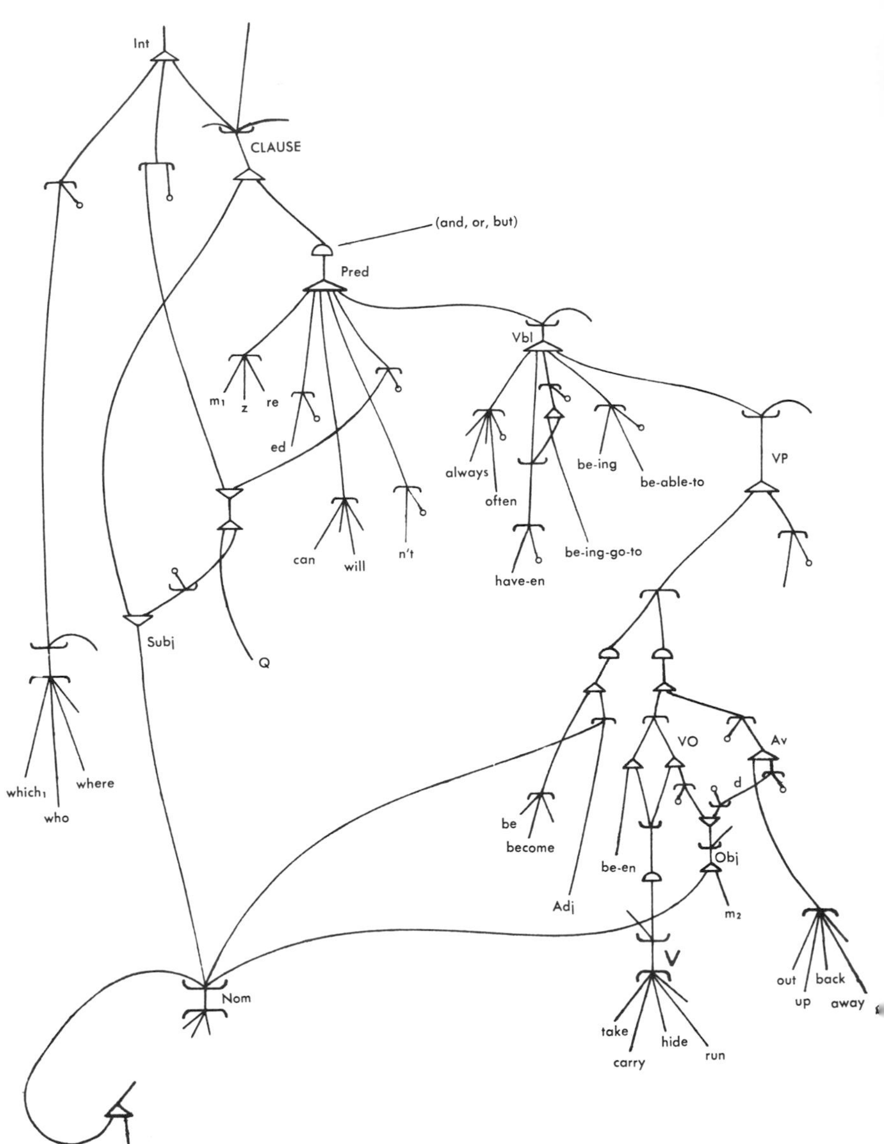

Figure 10. A Tentative Fragment of English Lexotactics.

Figure 10 is distinctive rather than optional. The subject line leading downward from the clause construction to nominals (*Nom*) encounters an upward AND which, if the interrogative lexeme ᴸ/Q/ is present (and only then), delays a downward subject impulse until after the occurrence of ᴸ/Q/, and thus until after the first part of the predicate construction. When ᴸ/Q/ is not present, the order is that seen in *Johnny can play the saxophone;* but when ᴸ/Q/ occurs, it precedes the subject and, in the encoding

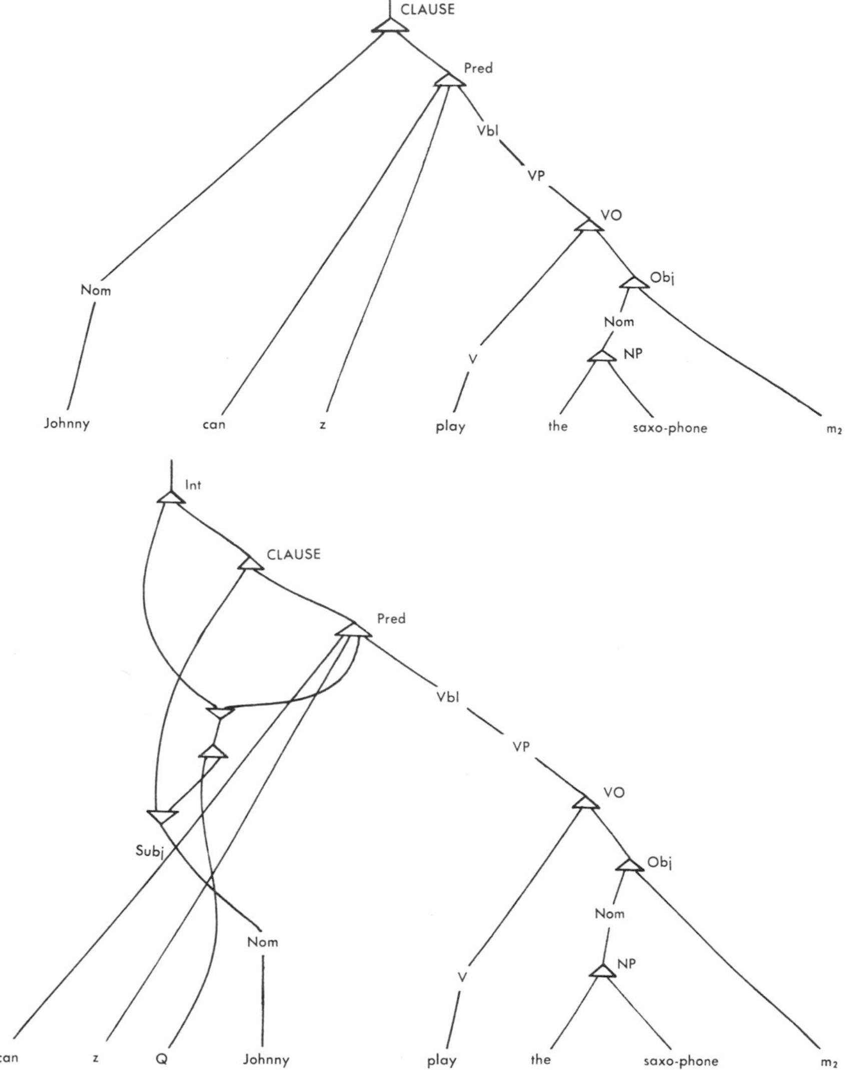

Figure 11.

process, the impulse going from the clause construction to the subject phrase is delayed until the impulse comes from the predicate construction to the other line connecting to this upward AND; the resulting order is that seen in *Can Johnny play the saxaphone?* (Figure 11). The lexeme L/Q/ is itself realized as M/Ø/ in this example (because M/can/ is present), but in some environments (as specified in the morphotactics) it is realized as *do,* as in *Does Johnny know any other songs?*

Figure 10 introduces a new type of node, the COORDINATION element, represented by a half circle. A downward impulse meeting this element may optionally result in two or more separate impulses continuing downward from it, each of which is treated by the morphotactics as if it were the only one. In the algebraic notation the coordination element may be represented by an asterisk, together with identification in parentheses of any units which may occur between the last two of the coordinate units; for example, the coordination element above the *Pred* construction in Figure 10 might be represented in the formula for *CLAUSE* as follows:

CLAUSE / Subj *(and,or,but)Pred

One of the phenomena often associated with the coordination element is another type of interstratal discrepancy, MULTIPLE REALIZATION. Multiple realization is present when a unit has two or more separate realizations on the next lower stratum. The coordination element is discussed further below (under Grammar).

One further type of relationship, involving a special type of neutralization, is REDUPLICATION. There are two types of reduplication element, one for anticipating a following unit, the other for repeating a preceding unit They may be represented graphically by triangles attached to lines, at the left (for ANTICIPATORY REDUPLICATION) or at the right (for REPETITIONAL). An example of anticipatory reduplication in the phonemic system of Monachi is shown in Figure 12. This example concerns the distributive prefix, and the graph accounts for its realization as P/paʾ/ in P/paʾpaya/ 'water here and there' (cf. P/paya/ 'water'), as P/noʾ/ in P/noʾnopiʾ/ 'houses here and there' (cf. P/nopiʾ/ 'house'), etc. A reduplication element may be represented algebraically by an equals sign (=) followed (for anticipatory) or preceded (for repetitional) by the label for the line to which the reduplication element is attached. Thus the reduplication element for the reduplicative consonant of Figure 12, or the line leading into it, may be represented as =C. A downward impulse going into the anticipatory reduplication element proceeds downward and makes the same choice at the downward OR that the next impulse to reach it will make Thus the impulse coming down from the higher stratum, which (by reaching an upward AND in the knot pattern) selects one of the possibilities makes its selection for two successive impulses coming down from th

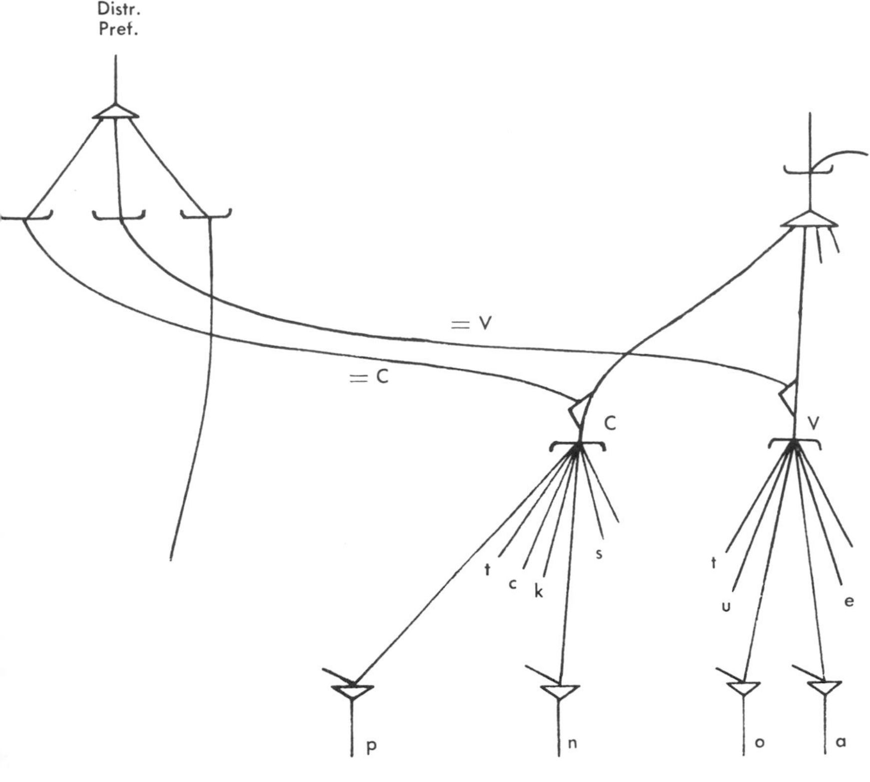

Figure 12. Reduplication in Monachi.

tactics. This is the special property of the reduplication element. (It would be possible to account for reduplication without the use of a special element, but only at considerable expense of ordinary AND and OR nodes; whether the reduplication element is to be regarded as a shorthand device for the more complex structure of AND and OR nodes, an element of structures of individual languages whose analysis in terms of ordinary lines and nodes belongs to linguistic theory, or a separate element in general linguistic theory as well, remains an open question for the present.) Reduplication occurs not only in phonology, but also in morphemic and lexemic systems. Also, there may be distinguished from each other the type of reduplication which realizes a unit of the upper stratum, as in the example of Figure 12, and the type which exists within a single tactic pattern; i.e., which is determined by the tactics itself rather than by the upper stratum. The latter type is present in the lexotactics of various Indo-European languages; case-number-gender suffixes of adjectives are reduplicatives whic repeat or anticipate the suffixes of the modified nouns. In English only trace of this type of concord remains, namely the agreement in number o certain determiners with nouns (see Appendix).

Phonology

The few remarks given here concerning the treatment of phonology i the current version of stratificational theory constitute only a brief intro duction to and commentary upon a more detailed exposition given else where (Lamb 1966b).

The distinction between the (basic) phonemic and hypophonemic strat has generally been overlooked in the past. The classical phoneme o Bloomfieldian and neo-Bloomfieldian linguistics was on the stratum whic is called hypophonemic here, but its size is that of the unit here called th (basic) phoneme. That is, the classical phoneme, as was recognized som years ago by Hockett (1947a, 1947b, 1955), is not a structural elemen of language. Rather, it is a conflation of two separate types of combinatio of elementary units: (1) the hypophonemic realization of the (basic phoneme, and (2) a tactically defined unit of a certain rank in the hypo phonotactics. Hockett took it to be only the latter, but the former im portant structural relationship, although it was quite generally overlooked evidently exerted a strong subconscious influence on linguists' thinking This conflation is similar to that associated with the term *word,* which ha been used in connection with both (1) the morphemic realization of th lexeme and (2) a unit of a certain important rank in morphotactics. Th conflation was possible since, in both cases, the two units often coincide But more important is that they often fail to coincide.

The stratum whose eme is the phonological segment and whose tactic specifies the structure of syllables and phonological words is that calle (basic) phonemic here. The stratum having these properties was gen erally thought to be the same as that specified by the various classica principles concerning distinctiveness, complementary distribution, biunique ness, and the like (Swadesh 1934, Twaddell 1935, Hockett 1942, Bloc 1948, 1950); but the latter is the hypophonemic. That is, the classica phonemic level is here split into two separate strata, with distinct tacti patterns and alternation patterns (Lamb 1966b). The tactics of the hypo phonemic stratum of a language specifies how hypophonemes (i.e. phono logical components) are arranged in segments and clusters. This specifica tion includes that of conditioning environments for those types o "morphophonemic" alternation which involve phonological component As the hypophonemic and (basic) phonemic systems both have alternatio patterns, there are two separate alternation patterns corresponding t classical morphophonemics. (Or, by that definition of morphophonemics which allowed it to be concerned with all alternation in the classical phonemic shapes of classical morphemes, there are three separate alternation patterns, the lexonic, the morphonic, and the phononic.) The morphon corresponds approximately to the classical morphophoneme. The morphonic alternation pattern (part of the phonemic system) is concerned with alternation among (basic) phonemes — i.e. alternation involving phonological segments — while the phononic alternation pattern specifies alternations involving phonological components.

As mentioned above, the hypophonemic system seems to lack a sign pattern, at least one of the type found in higher stratal systems; and it is at the level where a hypophonemic sign pattern might be expected that the transition is to be recognized between linguistic structure and its external manifestations, articulatory, acoustic, and auditory (Lamb 1966b).

Grammar

The distinction between the morphemic stratum and the lexemic has likewise been overlooked or else haphazardly treated in the past. Figure 3 above, showing part of the lexemic sign pattern of English, indicates one of the types of evidence for the separation. The two strata also have quite different tactic patterns, as illustrated in the Appendix. This difference in tactics is the source of the traditional morphology-syntax division, but it has usually been supposed that the distinction was based merely on the size of units dealt with, and the existence of a sign pattern and an alternation pattern between the two tactic patterns generally went unrecognized. The unit whose combinations are defined by the syntax (i.e. lexotactics) is actually not the word but the lexeme. To suppose that syntax should deal with combinations of words (or that the tactics of syllable structure should be based upon the classical phoneme) would be to make the same mistake as that involved in supposing that morphological structure should deal with combinations of syllables.

The common view put forth in opposition to supporters of a morphology-syntax distinction has been that there is a single morphotactics, concerned with combinations of morphemes up to the tactic level of the sentence (e.g. Hjelmslev 1943, Harris 1951). The structural unit taken as the basis of this conflation of tactic patterns, called the morpheme by American structuralists, commonly approximated that which is here called the lexon, a unit as appropriate as could be expected for such a compromise since it is intermediate between the morpheme and the lexeme.

Properties of morphemic and lexemic structure are exemplified in the Appendix. A special feature of the lexotactics of English and other languages, possibly not found at lower strata, is the coordination element, represented graphically by a half circle. This element provides the option for an impulse moving downward to result in two or more separate downward impulses, with an intervening conjunction between the last two; and each such impulse is treated by the next lower tactic pattern as if it were the only one. A configuration that would allow a downward impulse to result, optionally, in two or more, with a conjunction between the last two, can easily be constructed from AND and OR elements, as shown in Figure 13. But the coordination element is recognized as a separate entity since (1) it is so recurrent that its internal analysis can efficiently be treated as a part of linguistic theory rather than as a highly repetitive part of the description of individual languages; and (2) it has a special property not provided for in the analysis shown in Figure 13, namely that each impulse going down from the coordination element is treated as if it were occurring individually with the preceding and following units in its environment. The significance

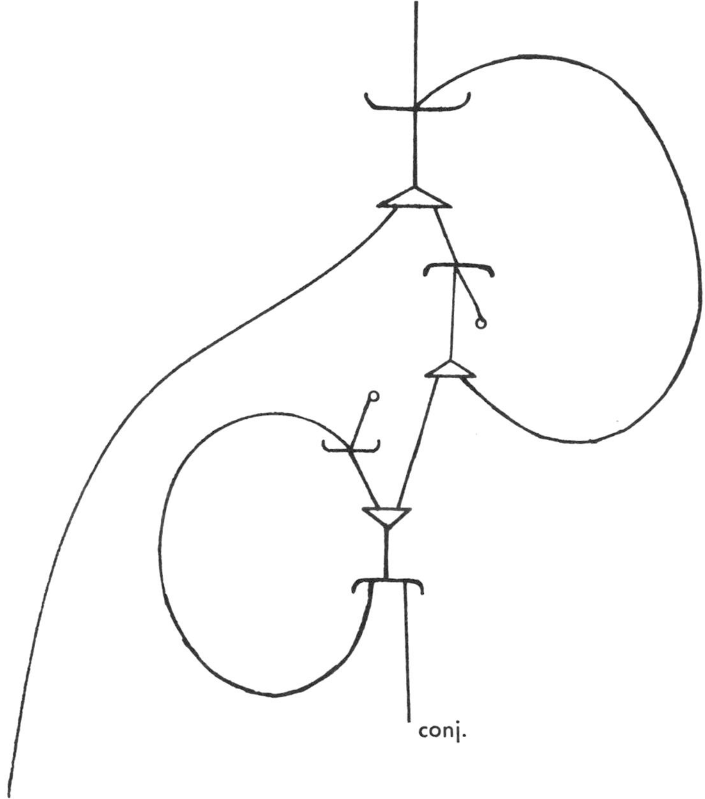

Figure 13.

of this property is perhaps best understood with the aid of an example. In the lexemic combination

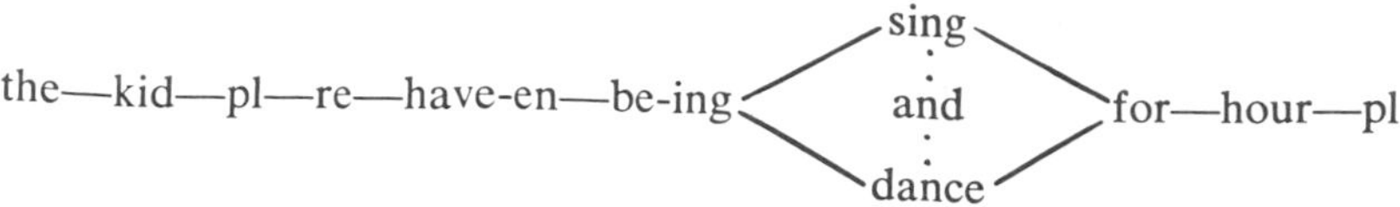

the kids have been singing and dancing for hours,

the lexemes ^{L}/sing/ and ^{L}/dance/ each occur with preceding ^{L}/be-ing/ and following ^{L}/for hour pl/. Such a non-linear combination, however, is unacceptable to the morphotactics, which arranges the realizations of the coordinate elements sequentially; but each of these realizations occurs in the morphemic realization of its environment, up to the limits of a morphological construction. Thus the lexon ^{LN}/ing/, a component of ^{L}/be-ing/, is multiply realized on the morphemic stratum:

^{M}/ . . . have # be -en # sing -ing # and # dance -ing . . ./

Examples of various other features of the lexemic and morphemic systems of English are given in the Appendix.

Semology

Semological structure still presents a number of unsolved and partly solved problems. It is only during the current period that the need for two separate strata in semology is becoming clear. In part this new stratal distinction could be described as the discovery of a new stratum intermediate between the former lexemic and sememic strata; some phenomena formerly assigned to the lexemic system are now seen as belonging to the sememic. The assortment of various semological phenomena among the patterns of the two stratal systems is at present tentative and in part uncertain.

It is probably true for every language that the sememic sign pattern has considerably more portmanteau realization than lower sign patterns; but there are also numerous instances of composite realization. Examples of composite realization in the English sememic system (i.e. sememic signs with two or more semons as downward components) are: ^{SS}/give-up/, ^{SS}/go-through-with/, ^{SS}/go-in-for/, ^{SS}/kick-the-bucket/.

Investigations associated with the term *componential analysis* (cf. Hammel et al. 1965 and other works referred to there) have concerned three separate types of structure belonging in three different parts of the sememic system: portmanteau realization (in the upper part of the sign pattern), alternation, and taxonomic structure (in the tactic pattern). Kinship terminologies (Lounsbury 1956, 1964a, 1964b, Goodenough 1956, Wallace and Atkins 1960, Conklin 1964, Hammel et al. 1965) offer the best known examples of portmanteau realization in the sememic system. They also exemplify phenomena of the sememic alternation pattern. The outstanding feature relating to a kinship terminology in the sememic alternation pattern is zero realization. Various hypersemons, e.g. those for sex of cousins and relative age of siblings in English, commonly fail to get realized sememically since they are not accommodated by the semotactics (Lamb 1965b). Those which are accommodated are realized as sememes, and these are the (upward) components of the sememic signs, which are realized as kinship terms. (The sememes and sememic signs were called *basic sememes* and *sememes,* respectively, in the terminology of Lamb 1965b.) Zero realization of kinship hypersemons has been treated in detail (in different terms) by Lounsbury (1964a, 1964b, 1965).

Taxonomic structure is to be clearly distinguished from that present in the alternation and sign patterns. Taxonomic hierarchies (Frake 1961, Conklin 1962) belong to the semotactics, and their various categories and levels of contrast are structurally significant precisely by virtue of their distributional properties, i.e. their properties of co-occurrence with other sememes.

Semotactics differs from lower tactic patterns not only in incorporating considerably more hierarchial taxonomic configurations but also in the presence of considerably more upward ANDS. An upward AND in a tactic pattern represents the occurrence of a unit in two or more tactic functions at the same time. (An upward OR represents alternative, rather than simultaneous, tactic functions.) Thus semotactic arrangements do not have immediate constituent structure in the usual sense, and they cannot in general be represented by tree diagrams.

Some Earlier Views of Linguistic Structure

Various pre- and quasi-stratificational views of linguistic structure, and earlier forms of stratificational theory, can be distinguished from one another on the basis of how many of the stratal distinctions were recognized by them and how the various structural relationships of stratal systems were treated.

Much of the thinking and discussion of linguists during the past few decades has been devoted to the concepts of phoneme and morpheme and the relationships between the units having these designations. As mentioned above, the term *phoneme* has usually been used for segments on the hypophonemic stratum. Many linguists in the past considered the morpheme to be a combination of phonemes, and they recognized no element of any higher stratum. They were thus holding a monostratal view of linguistic structure. Although the untenability of the concept of the morpheme as a combination of phonemes was demonstrated many times over a period of years (e.g. Harris 1942) it remained a remarkably persistent notion, revalent even into the decade of the sixties. This concept was often held ide by side with several others, so that the term *morpheme* was used for a vide variety of different units, sometimes within the pages of a single book.

A very widely held concept of the morpheme has been that it is a class f combinations of classical phonemes, called its allomorphs. But this conept too is untenable. For a class can be completely specified by a listing or other precise identification) of its members; this is not true of any of he units that linguists have wanted to call morphemes, since their specificaion requires not only an identification of their realizations but also the nformation as to the environments that provide the conditions for the ccurrence of the realizations. This concept also runs into logical difficulties ecause of the phenomena of empty realization (cf. Hockett 1947c), portnanteau realization (cf. Hockett 1947c, Nida 1948), "link phonemes" Wells 1949), and the type of problem exemplified by the past tense of English *take* (Bloch 1947, Nida 1948, Hockett 1954). To take account f empty realization with the morpheme as a class would mean recognizing ntities which are members of nonexistent classes; no version of set theory ccommodates such a notion. The opposite relationship, zero realization, vould involve classes with no members, and this is a part of set theory i.e. the empty set); but empty realization violates the concept of the class. he same is true of the portmanteau, since it would involve an entity being member simultaneously of two classes, but only when they are concateated. This is not the same as the relationship of membership in two or nore separate classes. That concept, which is allowable in set theory, vould be the relationship of neutralization (i.e. upward OR), if the class oncept of the morpheme were tenable.

These difficulties led Hockett to the position that phonemes and norphemes are on different strata and that morphemes are REPRESENTED y combinations of phonemes, rather than having these combinations as nembers (Hockett 1954). Hockett's morpheme, during this period, was pproximately the same as the unit here called the lexon. This improved onception was still deficient in that it assigned no structural status to norphophonemes or to alternations among phonemes independently of norphemes, and in that, as Hockett pointed out (1954), it failed to proide a thoroughly realistic and economical account of the forms like English *ook*.

A further development of Hockett's two stratum view (1961) replaced he earlier concept of representation by a more complex relationship, "is rogrammed into", to allow for more economical handling of certain henomena, but he still refrained from giving a structural status to the norphophoneme.

A move toward the recognition of a third stratum intermediate between hat of the "morphemes" (lexons) and classical phonemes was made by

Trager (1955) in his use of a descriptive framework that (like Hockett's "programmed into" relationship) allowed morphemes to have allomorphs which in turn were subject to morphophonemic rules. But a complete intermediate stratum was not recognized by Trager, since the intermediate level was provided only for certain morphemes, while others were allowed to coexist with the allomorphs of the former.

Hjelmslev's glossematics, as presented in his *Prolegomena to a Theory of Language* (1943), came quite close to an explicit recognition of three separate strata. His basic division, like Hockett's, was into two parts, which he called content and expression. But within each a distinction was drawn between ideal chains and actualized chains, which Hjelmslev described as differing with respect to the relationship called neutralization in this Outline. Thus Hjelmslev might be said to have recognized a stratal distinction within both expression and content (cf. Lamb 1966a). His ideal chains in the expression plane are approximately at the morphonic level of the present system, while his actualized expression is comparable to the classical phonemic level. His actualized content chains are roughly at the morphemic level, and his ideal content is a conflation which includes features of lexons, lexemes, and sememes.

A complete intermediate stratum, called morphophonemic, was used in my dissertation, written in 1957, and other descriptions written at Berkeley in the late fifties (cf. Biligiri 1959, Barker 1964, Shipley 1964). The "morphemes" of this three-stratum system correspond to lexons of the present system, the "morphophonemes" to morphons except that their arrangements were those of the (basic) phonemes; and the "phonemes" were, like those of other linguists, segments on the hypophonemic stratum.

Some of the evidence for additional structure above the "morphemic" (lexonic) level was presented in Hockett's textbook (1958), in his discussion of "surface and deep grammar" and of units which he called "idioms" (some of which are lexemes, others sememes); but Hockett refrained from using this evidence to establish any higher strata.

Another approach toward the recognition of a stratum above the classical morphemic level was that of Harris's transformational analysis (1954, 1957), which has been developed in three different directions by Harris (1965), his student Chomsky (1957, 1965), and the Russian linguist Shaumyan (1965). This is a process approach, however, which actually has refrained from recognizing a separate higher stratum and instead has treated pairs of related syntactic combinations by deriving one from another by means of "transformations" (using a term borrowed from mathematics). The latest formulation of Chomsky's variety of transformational grammar (1965) approaches a stratal distinction in regarding "deep structure" and "surface structure" as different levels; but these levels are only partly separated since they share many features with each other, including even phonological features. His transformations are now conceived of as rules for converting from the level of deep structure to that of surface structure.

In 1960 I proposed the recognition of a stratum above the classical morphemic stratum, and a four stratum framework of linguistic structure.[1] The first edition of the *Outline of Stratificational Grammar* (1962a) recognized five strata, called phonemic, morphophonemic, morphemic, semomorphemic, and sememic. In 1963 and 1964 I reverted temporarily to a four stratum system and revised the terminology by introducing the terms with the suffix *-on* (1964b) and by calling the strata phonemic, morphemic, lexemic, and sememic. Gleason (1964) and I (1964a, 1964b) also made attempts to clarify the relationships which differentiate the strata from one another. Further clarification of the relationships present in stratal systems has been attempted in Lamb 1965b and Lamb 1966b.[2] In 1965 a framework with five stratal systems was used (Lamb 1965b), and the further move has now been made to three pairs of stratal systems.

An alternative to the concept of stratification in linguistic structure is the use of process description, involving various processes of "change" taking place in a fictional time span. According to this concept, which has had remarkably widespread use despite its lack of reality, the downward OR relationship is treated as a process, in which one of the alternatives is basic and is "replaced" by the other under some conditions while under other conditions it remains unchanged. Perhaps the essential difference between the process conception and that of structural relationships is that the former (when consistently used) recognizes only the two (or more) alternatives (corresponding to the lines leading down from the downward OR) while the latter recognizes also the single element above the OR relationship (corresponding to the line above the OR node), an element which is not the same as either (or any) of the alternants, but which "underlies" them both (or all).

The process way of thinking is similar to that indulged in by the many people who believe that man is descended from the ape. The more advanced view is of course that man and the ape are descended from a common ancestor which was not the same as either. The same type of misunderstanding is involved in the familiar view that Latin and Greek (and other Indo-European languages) are descended from Sanskrit. Similarly, beginning students in linguistics, when given their first exercise in comparative reconstruction from forms in two related languages, commonly try to derive the forms of language A from those of language B or vice versa, even after having been told that their job is to provide reconstructions for a proto-language that is not the same as either A or B.

Process description in synchronic linguistics has been most tenacious and widespread in connection with "morphophonemic" (i.e. morphonic and phononic) alternation; where there is recurrent alternation between two hypophonemic entities, it has been traditional for the linguist to say that one is derived from the other. Just as the man on the street recognizes only two entities, man and ape, and fails to consider the third, the common ancestor, so some linguists have recognized only the two alternating hypophonemic units and have ignored the third entity at a different, higher level of the structure, which "underlies" both but is not the same as either.

The morphophonemic process is commonly thought of as "replacement" of the one phonological unit by the other, but various other locutions are often used under the appropriate conditions. In the case of zero realization, one says that the unit "is lost"; *dissimilation, assimilation,* and other terms are taken over from the terminology of diachronic linguistics on the basis of an analogy with real processes of actual linguistic change which occur during the history of a language. In the minds of some linguists the analogy has been carried so far as to have become an actual confusion of diachronic processes with synchronic relationships.

Whereas the stratificational approach operates with a small number of stratal systems — with only two alternation patterns between morphons and hypophonemes — the process approach usually allows for an indefinitely large number of levels (i.e. periods in the fictional time span). Thus Chomsky (1964:71) declares that he used some twenty-five levels in his process description of Hebrew morphophonemics, "and this is surely an underestimate". The classical phonemic (i.e. hypophonemic) level, however, is none of these; for Chomsky (1964) and Halle (1959) find that level not only useless but also bothersome (cf. Lamb 1966b). This view of multiple levels none of which is the classical phonemic is not a reflection of the nature of linguistic structure but is rather a consequence of applying to that structure a method of description inappropriate to it.

Not to be confused with the type of process discussed above is the morphological process or grammatical process, an alternative treatment for an area which includes not only the morphemic alternation pattern but also morphotactics and part or all (depending upon the practicioner) of classical morphophonemics. Using the morphological process approach one describes the word as the result of applying one or more morphological processes, in succession, to a root (or to more than one root in the case of the process of compounding). The most common types of morphological process are prefixation (addition of a prefix) and suffixation (addition of a suffix). Also recognized are infixation, ablaut or internal change, and suppletion. The process of suppletion replaces a whole morpheme by another, as when *good* /gud/ is said to be replaced by /bet/ in *better.* (The more sophisticated approach is of course that which recognizes an underlying structural entity ^{LN}/good/ that is not the same as either /gud/ or /bet/.) Hockett (1955) has provided a framework which systematizes this approach and extends it to apply to forms larger than words, in a process version of the attempt to do away with the morphology-syntax distinction.

The morphological process approach requires the analyst to distinguish roots from affixes (i.e. prefixes, suffixes, and infixes). Its applicability to languages thus depends rather importantly upon the reality of such a distinction as a general property of linguistic structures. Although there have been a number of attempts to devise criteria which would allow the distinction to be made in borderline cases (e.g. Nida 1949:82-83, even though his system did not make use of morphological processes, Pittman 1948), none of them provides for unequivocal determination in all instances. An example of the difficulty is provided by some forms of Monachi. Given *wono* 'basket' and *wonowee* 'in the basket' the morphological process analyst would presumably regard the latter as resulting from a process of suffixation; and *tawono* 'our basket(s)' would be the result of adding the pronominal prefix *ta-*. Likewise, *tawonowee* 'in our basket(s)' presumably consists of a prefix, a root, and a suffix; i.e., a root to which have been applied both prefixation and suffixation. How, then, is *tawee* 'in us' to be described? To the linguist who operates with morphemes and morphotactics rather than with roots and affixation, the problem is nonexistent.

During the past ten years process description has been applied quite vigorously at a still higher level, at which the processes are called transformations. It has been said (at one time or another during this period) that passive sentences are "derived" from active ones by the passive transformation, that interrogative sentences are derived from declarative ones, and so forth. (Again there is a non-process, or stratificational, way of describing the same relationships, which recognizes a third entity, at the next higher stratum, underlying both the active and the passive, etc.)

One may distinguish several degrees of sophistication in the use of process description. The more naive versions never allow the "pre-process" forms to contain entities not found on the surface. Consider a typical student exercise in morphological analysis (such as Exercise 6 in this Outline), in which the left-hand column contains singular (or nominative or present-tense) forms of some language while the right-hand column consists of plural (or genitive or past tense) forms. The beginning student approaches such a problem as one of deriving the plural forms from the singular. At a slightly higher degree of sophistication the student recognizes that an alternative would be to derive the singular forms from the plural; i.e. he allows himself two alternatives and chooses that which gives the simpler description. At a still more advanced level is the type of description which, where economy will result, is willing to set up the stems in 'basic forms' which coincide sometimes with the singular forms and sometimes with the stems appearing in the plural forms. At the next higher level of sophistication is the approach which would (for the sake of a simple description) allow basic forms of some stems to be written so that they coincide with neither of the actually occurring forms, even though they are still written in terms of "phonemes" (cf. Nida 1949:34-35). Allowing himself this freedom the linguist sets up each basic form in such a way that the description of the processes yielding the actually occurring forms (i.e. the rewriting rules) will be as simple as possible. Even more advanced is the approach which allows some basic forms to contain phonological units that never actually occur as (classical) phonemes. Thus Panini's grammar of Sanskrit uses, for the sake of economy, a long vocalic *r* in some basic forms, even though only short vocalic *r* occurs in actual hypophonemic forms. Similarly, one means of treating English *knife:knives* (in which there is alternation in voicing of the spirant) along with *fife:fifes* and *hive:hives* is to make use of three separate phonological units underlying labial spirants in basic forms, even though only two are distinguished hypophonemically.

Finally, the highest degree of sophistication of process description may be called quasi-stratificational. Here the linguist realizes that he is dealing with different levels of structure, but he continues to use the method of description that is appropriate only to the process conception or to diachronic description. In classical morphophonemics the advance to this degree of sophistication was achieved sporadically but never became incorporated into general doctrine. Instead many neo-Bloomfieldians, recognizing the lack of psychological reality of process description, concluded during the forties that one must abandon economy in this area altogether, since it did not occur to them that any other means than process description was possible for dealing directly with morphophonemic alternation. Some linguists continued to use process morphophonemics at one of the degrees of sophistication, sometimes apologetically, while others took the view that morphophonemic alternation had no structural significance and instead was merely a matter of alternate phonemic shapes of morphemes; where a morphophonemic rule could be used in a description it was regarded as merely a means of summarizing or abbreviating several statements about allomorphs but was in itself considered to be without structural significance.

In using the quasi-stratificational process approach the linguist recognizes that there are separate strata but he states his rules in a way that would be appropriate to a pure process conception; i.e., as rewrite rules, which replace certain units under certain conditions. He thus fails to give explicit recognition to the third, underlying entity, except in occasional cases like that of the long vocalic *r* of Sanskrit. Given a particular alternation in a language between two units /x/ and /y/, where /y/ occurs, let us say, in some restricted environment and /x/ elsewhere (but suppose that the language also has forms with /y/ not participating in the alternation), then process descriptions of any of the degrees of sophistication would be the same; they would state (either in words or by means of a rewrite rule) that /x/ is replaced by (or rewritten as) /y/ in that restricted environment. It is understood in this type of description that *in other environments /x/ remains unchanged* (to use the common locution), which is to imply that *the (post-process) /x/ that alternates with /y/ is the same element as the underlying /x/ which is either replaced by /y/ or remains unchanged.*

A true stratificational description, on the other hand, recognizes a third entity, which is different from both /x/ and /y/, and there is no longer any process. Nothing — neither /x/ nor the underlying entity — ever gets replaced by (or rewritten as) /y/; instead all three entities exist simultaneously. Thus another difference between the two approaches is that there is no directionality in a stratificational description as there is in process descriptions, which move in a single direction. For example, Chomsky's (1964) phonology goes from syntactic representations to phonetic features; it is called "interpretive"; and no means is provided of accounting for the ability of speakers of a language to understand one another. A stratificational description, on the other hand, does not move in either direction. The structure is regarded as static, as a system of relationships, which may be traversed in either direction.

Another deficiency of process description (even at the highest degree of sophistication) is that it imposes a need for artificial ordering of the rewrite rules; i.e. ordering which has no structural significance and is necessary only because of the way rewrite rules operate. Thus Chomsky (1964: 84) cites the following ordered rewrite rules for Russian (restated from Trubetzkoy 1939):

(i) o → ọ in the context: — l

(ii) l → Ø in the context: Vowel — Nasal+Consonant

"Thus phonemic /sólncă/ ("sun") is phonetic [sọ́ncə] . . . the rules must be ordered as given." This ordering is needed only because the rules are rewrite rules, i.e. rules which replace the entities being rewritten, so that they are no longer available to serve as conditioning environments. If the situation is described in terms of realization of higher level units by lower level units (rather than replacement), there is no need for ordering; nothing happens to the higher level units; rather, their realizations "appear;" and the "rules" can occupy the same level of ordering in the description.

The artificial ordering required in a process description must of course be distinguished from real ordering, i.e. that which has structural significance. The most important type of structurally significant ordering is that related to stratification itself; an alternation at one stratum is at a different part of the structure from alternations at the next lower stratum; in a process description the rule(s) for the former would precede those for the latter. Another important type of real or structural ordering is that within the downward ordered OR (treated in Lamb 1964a as ordering of subrules of a realization rule). These three types of ordering (one artificial, two real) are conflated in a process description, even at the quasi-stratificational degree of sophistication; all are treated as ordering of rewrite rules.

One further disadvantage of process description is of rather drastic significance for the overall economy of the description: since there is no sharp distinction drawn between units of different levels — i.e. since units remain unchanged when not rewritten and hence exist at both the upper level and the lower — and since phonological units at lower strata have components (or distinctive features), units of higher levels must also consist of phonological components. Thus Chomsky (1965) introduces his binary distinctive features at the level of "deep structure," i.e. even "before" the transformations.

In general, the essence of the process approach is to produce a linguistic form and then to change it into another, then into another, etc. In a stratificational framework, on the other hand, the decisions leading to the form that will finally appear are made before any form is produced. In the various alternation patterns, tactic patterns, etc. there are no linguistic forms at all; the linguistic structure consists entirely of relationships. Impulses move through the network of relationships and only at its "lower" end are objects produced, after all the decisions have been made as to what these objects will be.

Notes to Chapter II

[1] This proposal was presented in my paper "The Strata of Linguistic Structure", delivered at the annual meeting of the Linguistic Society of America, Hartford, December, 1960. Further evidence for the fourth stratum was given in "On the Nature of the Sememe" delivered at the summer 1961 meeting of the Linguistic Society of America, Austin, July, 1961. The latter paper was incorporated, in revised form, in Lamb 1964b.

[2] To properly relate to one another my papers of the past few years one must distinguish dates of publication from dates of writing. The order in which my papers relating to stratificational theory were written is as follows: 1961, 1962b, 1962a, 1964b, 1964a, 1966d, 1965a, 1966c, *in press,* 1965b, 1966a, 1966b.

III. LINGUISTIC DESCRIPTION

It is vain to do with more what can be done with fewer.

William of Occam

A linguistic description conveys certain effective information about a linguistic structure, and to do so it uses a certain amount of surface information. In describing (part of) a linguistic structure the grammarian should try to present a maximum of effective information with a minimum of surface information. There are various operations which can be performed upon a preliminary or tentative description to simplify it, i.c. to reduce its surface information without alteration of its effective information.

Two descriptions convey the same effective information if they account for (or predict) the same data. This concept can be specified more precisely as follows.

Effective Information

A TOP LINE of a linguistic graph is a line at the top of the graph; i.e. a line of the graph which does not lead upward to any other line of the graph. For example, the top lines of a graph of a morphonic alternation pattern represent morphons. Similarly, a BOTTOM LINE of a graph is a line of the graph which does not lead downward to any other line of the graph.

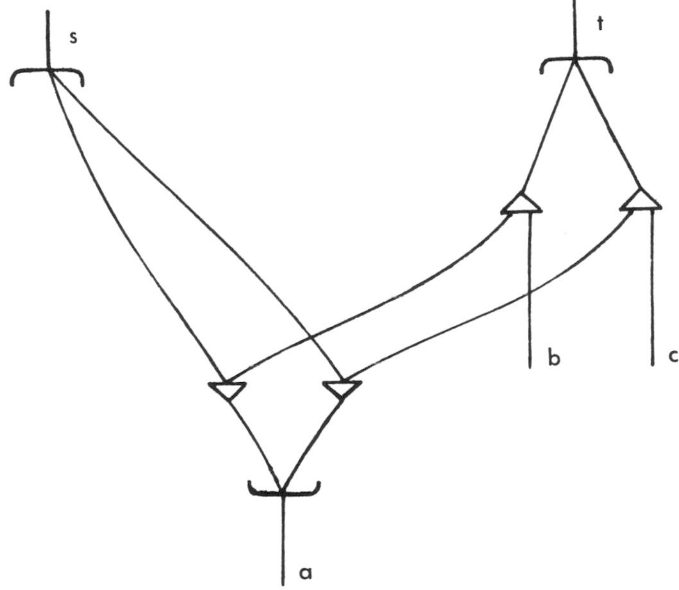

Figure 14.

A LINE-ACTIVATION is an individual instance of activation of a line, i.e. a movement of a single impulse along it.

If *t* is a top line of a linguistic graph *G*, then a DOWNWARD OUTPUT OF *t* THROUGH *G* is a specific combination of (one or more) line-activations of bottom lines of *G* that can result from a downward impulse along *t*. Similarly, if *b* is a bottom line of *G*, then an UPWARD OUTPUT OF *b* THROUGH *G* is a specific combination of (one or more) line activations of top lines of *G* that can result from an upward impulse along *b*.

If a linguistic graph *G* has two or more top lines t_1, t_2, . . ., then any combination of them may be said to have one or more downward outputs through *G*. A specific combination of (one or more) line-activations of bottom lines of *G* that can result from a combination *T* of (one or more) downward impulses along one or more top lines is a DOWNWARD OUTPUT OF *T* THROUGH *G*. Similarly, a specific combination of (one or more) line-activations of top lines of *G* that can result from a combination *B* of (one or more) upward impulses along one or more bottom lines is an UPWARD OUTPUT OF *B* THROUGH *G*. For example, $^{D}a\ ^{D}b$ (i.e. ^{D}a followed by ^{D}b) is a downward output of $^{D}s \cdot {}^{D}t$ (i.e. ^{D}s and ^{D}t simultaneously) through the graph of Figure 14; another downward output of $^{D}s \cdot {}^{D}t$ is $^{D}a\ ^{D}c$. It is convenient to adopt the notational convention of writing simply *xy* rather than $^{D}x\ ^{D}y$ or $^{U}x\ ^{U}y$ for activation of a line *x* followed by activation of a line *y*. Similarly, $x \cdot y$ may be written for simultaneous activation of *x* and *y*. Using this convention, we may write $s \cdot t$ as the upward output of *ab* through the graph of Figure 14. The combination *ba* has no upward output through this graph, since no line-activations of top lines can result from *ba;* likewise, *b* has no upward output through this graph.

With respect to a graph *G*, the set of all possible downward outputs of a combination *T* of (one or more) downward impulses along one or more top lines of *G* is the DOWNWARD SET OF *T* THROUGH *G*. Similarly, the set of all possible upward outputs of a combination *B* of upward impulses along one or more bottom lines of *G* is the UPWARD SET OF *B* THROUGH *G*. For example, the downward set of *A* through the graph of Figure 15 has the members *abc, ac, ab, dbc, dc,* and *e*. The upward set of *abc* has the single member *A*. The upward set of *a* is empty, since *a* has no upward output.

A graph *G* may be considered as an alternative to another graph *H* if it is the same as *H* with respect to its bottom lines and its top lines. For example, two graphs of a tactic pattern may be considered as alternatives if their bottom lines connect to all the same emes and if they each have one top line connecting to a zero element. But two alternative graphs are not necessarily alike with respect to either effective information or surface information.

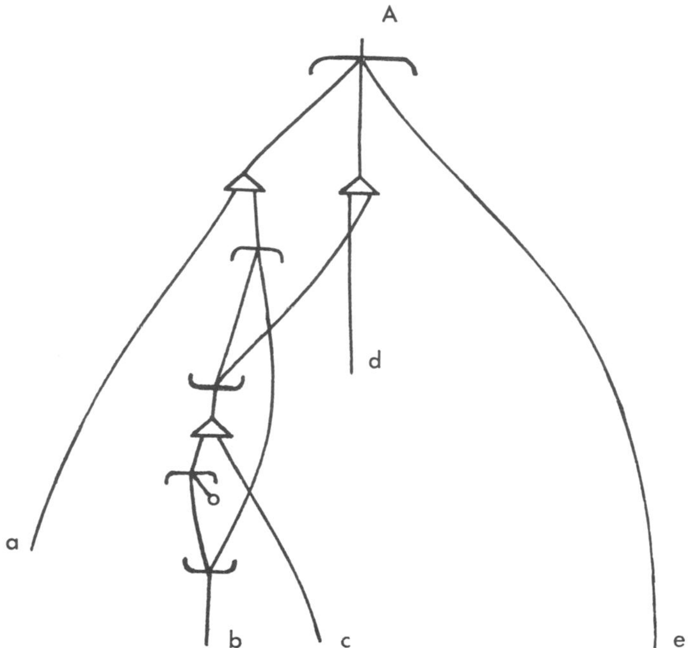

Figure 15.

Two graphs G and H which are alternatives to each other (i.e. have the same bottom lines and top lines) CONVEY THE SAME EFFECTIVE INFORMATION if and only if (1) for any combination T of downward impulses along top lines of G and H, the downward set of T through G is the same as the downward set of T through H, and (2) for any combination B of upward impulses along bottom lines of G and H, the upward set of B through G is the same as the upward set of B through H. If G conveys the same effective information as H, it may be said to be EQUIVALENT to H, and the rela-

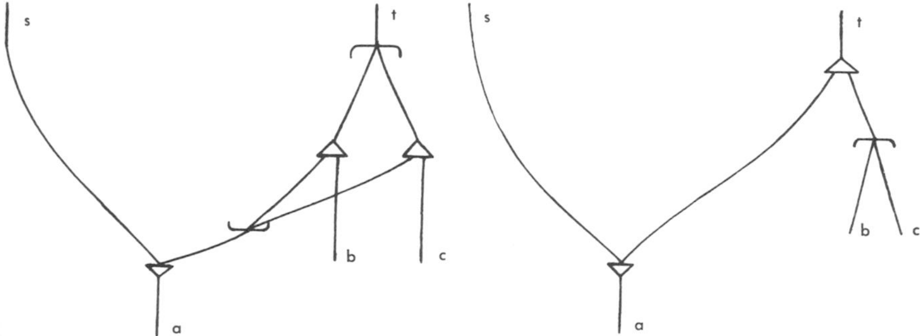

Figure 16.

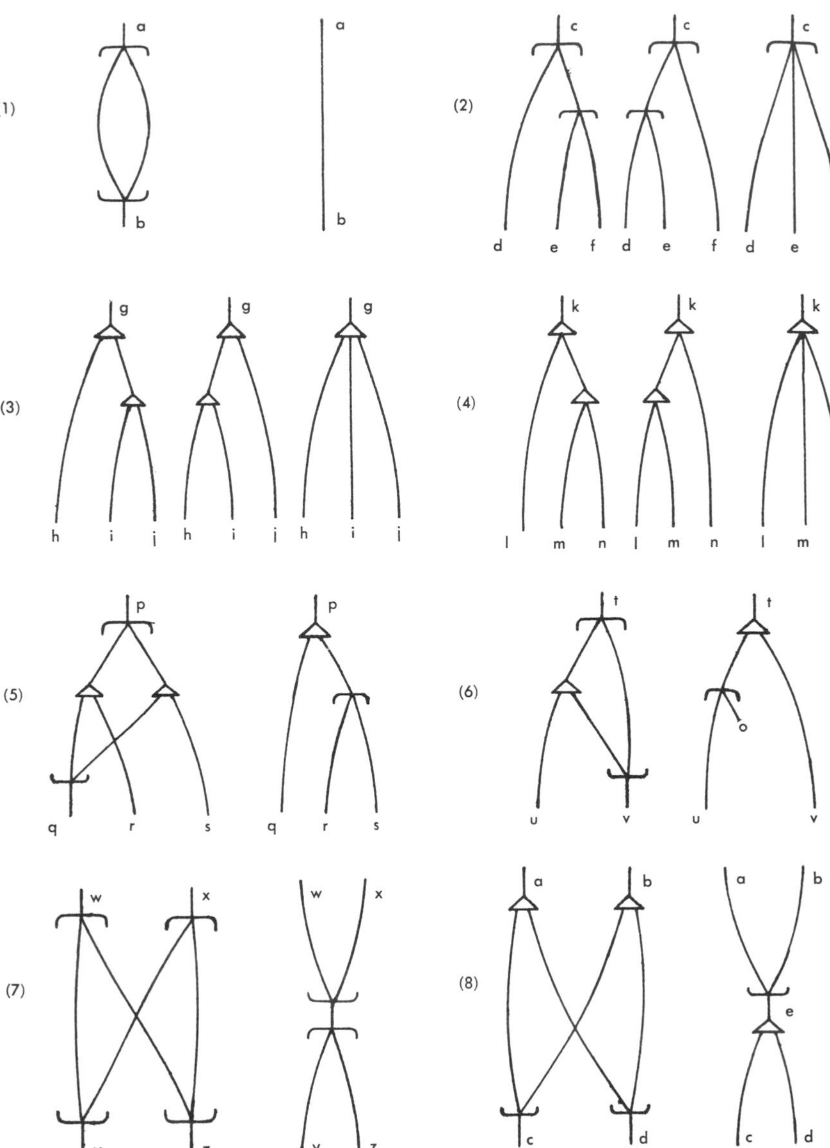
(1)
a
b
a
b
(2)
c
d
e
f
c
d
e
f
c
d
e
f
(3)
g
h
i
j
g
h
i
j
g
h
i
j
(4)
k
l
m
n
k
l
m
n
k
l
m
n
(5)
p
q
r
s
p
q
r
s
(6)
t
u
v
t
o
u
v
(7)
w
x
y
z
w
x
y
z
(8)
a
b
c
d
a
b
e
c
d

Figure 17.

tionship may be symbolized by the equivalence sign: $G \equiv H$. As an example, the two graphs of Figure 16 are equivalent to each other and to that of Figure 14.

These three graphs, however, differ from one another in surface information. That at the right in Figure 16 is clearly the simplest, i.e. has the least surface information. It does with fewer what the others do with more. It incorporates a generalization, while the others are repetitive, in that they express certain relationships separately which the simpler one states only once; the repetition constitutes their excess surface information.

In Figure 17 the graphs within each set convey the same effective information but differ in surface information (except that in sets 2 and 4 the first two graphs have the same surface information). In algebraic notation the examples may be described as follows (the numbering follows that of the figure):

(1) a / b,b ≡ a / b
(2) c / d,(e,f) ≡ c / (d,e),f ≡ c / d,e,f
(3) g / h (i j) ≡ g / (h i) j ≡ g / h i j
(4) k / l · (m · n) ≡ k / (l · m) · n ≡ k / l · m · n
(5) p / qr,qs ≡ p / q(r,s)
(6) t / uv,v ≡ t / [u]v
(7) w /y,z and x / y,z ≡ w,x / y,z
(8) a / cd and b / cd ≡ a,b / cd

To this list of equivalences may be added several quite similar ones, such as:

(9) c / d+(e+f) ≡ c / (d+e)+f ≡ c / d+e+f
(10) p / qs,rs ≡ p / (q,r)s
(11) p / q·r,q·s ≡ p / q · (r,s)
(12) p / q·s,r·s ≡ p / (q,r) · s
(13) t / u,uv ≡ t / u[v]

These simple equivalences, and other comparable ones, are derivable from the definition of equivalence given above. They may be regarded as rules for operations that may be performed upon a tentative description to reduce its surface information without altering its effective information; or, they can be used to compare alternative descriptions to determine whether or not they convey the same effective information: if the one description can be converted to the other through the use of these (and similar) rules, they are equivalent.

An additional type of equivalence is that which involves the ordered OR relationship. In Figure 18, the second graph has an ordered OR corresponding to an unordered OR in the first; this ordering allows the section at the right in the second graph to be simpler than the corresponding section of

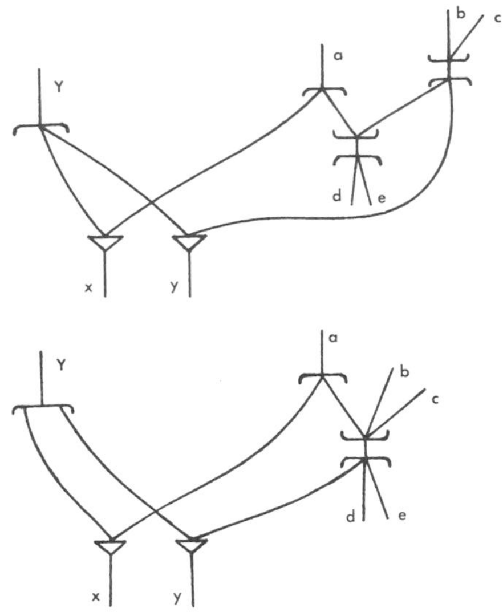

Figure 18.

the first. The situation shown is typical of alternations; the section at right is that part of the tactic pattern which specifies the conditions for the occurrence of the alternants. Of the alternants *x* and *y*, realizations of *Y*, *x* occurs in a restricted environment.

Surface Information

Two graphs which differ in amount of surface information may be said to differ in simplicity. The simpler graph is that which has less surface information. It is not necessarily preferable to the less simple one, however, since the two graphs may differ in effective information. But if two graphs have the same effective information and differ in surface information, then the simpler is to be preferred. It incorporates one or more generalizations absent from the more complicated one. The latter is more complicated because it repeats certain information presented only once in the simpler graph; it may thus be regarded as not presenting the full truth, in that at one or more places it treats a fact as if it were two or more separate facts.

To apply this principle of simplicity with greater precision it is necessary to have a means of measuring the quantity of surface information in a graph. It might be supposed that the number of nodes in a graph constitutes a satisfactory measure, but this possibility can easily be rejected; in Figure 19 the graph at left has fewer nodes but is clearly more complicated than that at the right. Another possibility would be the number of lines; this measure is suitable for grossly different alternatives, but in more

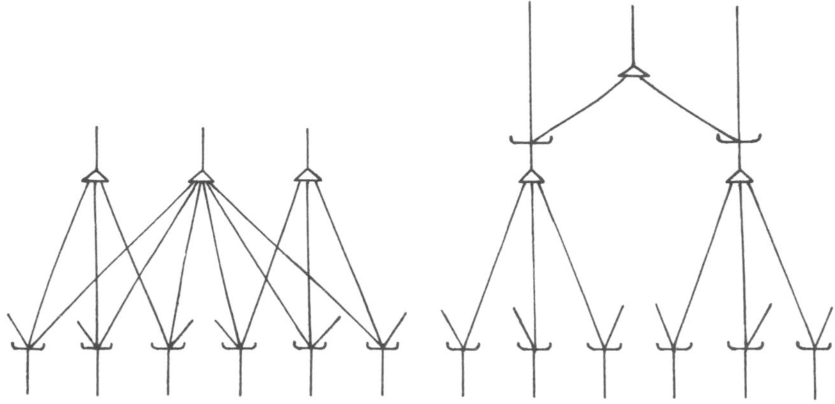

Figure 19.

refined analysis it too fails, for it turns out that not all lines express the same amount of information. In Figure 20 the alternatives have the same number of lines as well as the same number of nodes (and they convey

Figure 20.

the same effective information). But the graph at left is repetitive while that at right is economical in treating the fact that *a* leads down to *x*. The algebraic representation of the two graphs is:

a / x,xyz
a / x[yz]

Note also that if the situation is altered very slightly to that of Figure 21, the simpler graph has more lines as well as more nodes.

Thus a more refined measure of surface information is needed. The information that is actually relevant is just that which is needed to specify an individual linguistic structure, i.e. to distinguish it from all other linguistic structures. A brief discussion of just what kind of information this

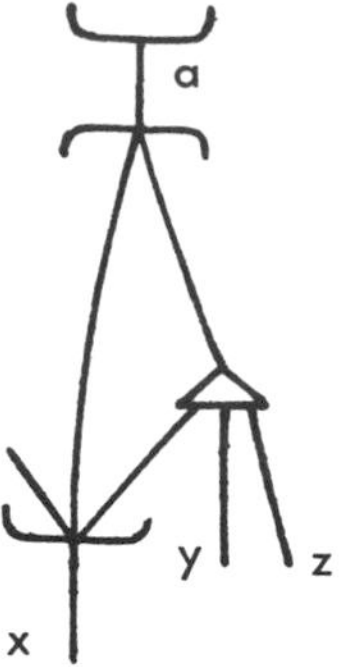

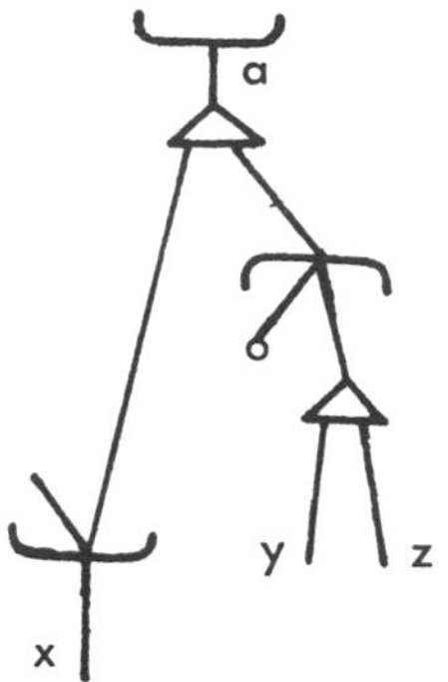

Figure 21.

is will help to explain the motivation for the measure of surface information defined below.

The information needed to distinguish a particular linguistic structure from all others is of course quite different from that which would in itself completely characterize a language, or distinguish it from all other phenomena in the universe. One must accept Hjelmslev's (1943) principle that the description of an individual language can be properly constructed only in the context of a general linguistic theory. That theory should specify the properties which all languages have in common, and the theory of the individual language constitutes only the supplementary information needed to specify the additional properties which make that particular instance of language different from any other.

What are the general properties of linguistic structure? Chapter II of this Outline attempts to identify the most important of them. It would appear that all languages are made up of stratal systems (although they do not necessarily all have the same number), that every stratal system is composed of certain patterns, each having certain characteristic configurations of relationships. In fact, graphs of the structures of two quite different languages, say English and Swahili, would look more alike than different on casual inspection, like two sheep in a herd; and only a highly skilled observer would be able to determine which was which. Thus every language has a morphemic sign pattern, with some two or three thousand or more downward ANDS and a few dozen upward ORS below them, and with lines connecting the ANDS to the ORS. This much is universal, and this much of the characterization of the structure of English and Swahili is given by linguistic theory. To define the morphemic sign pattern of a particular language it is necessary to specify which lines leading down from the ANDS connect to which ORS; i.e. (aside from portmanteau realization) it is the specific connections between these ANDS and ORS that distinguish the morphemic sign pattern of one language from that of another. And in general, the types of configurations and the approximate quantities of elements in any pattern of any stratal system are general properties shared by other languages; and the characterization of the individual linguistic structure requires only a specification of the precise connections. The surface information which the grammarian wants to minimize is this "connective" information.

The lines of a graph represent "connective" information, but different lines represent different amounts of such information. The following definitions lead to a measure of surface information which takes account of that fact.

The upward side of a downward AND or OR node is its SINGULAR SIDE, and the downward side is its PLURAL SIDE. Similarly, the downward side of an upward AND or OR node is its SINGULAR SIDE, and the upward side is its PLURAL SIDE.

In general, a line is INTERNAL if it connects (1) the singular sides of any two nodes, (2) the singular side of an unordered AND to the plural side of an ordered AND, (3) the singular side of an unordered OR to the plural side of an ordered OR, (4) the singular side of an OR to the plural side of an AND. Actually, for all of these situations except (4) the convention may be adopted of not writing the internal line at all. The types of internal lines are shown in the top row of Figure 22, and below each configuration which allows the possibility of using this convention, the corresponding reduced form is shown. These reduced forms might be regarded

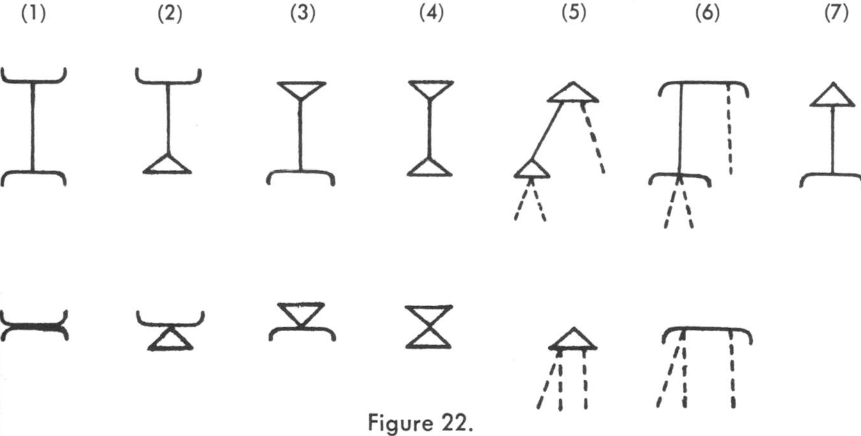

Figure 22.

as additional types of nodes. Those of (5) and (6), so regarded, involve only a slight modification of the definitions of the ordered AND and OR nodes.

In the configurations (1), (2), (3), and (4), the internal lines may be regarded as not expressing any connective information since identification of (a) connection to the singular side of a node plus (b) connections from its plural side to other nodes gives no further information than is provided by (b) alone. This same consideration applies to the connection from the plural side of an AND to the singular side of an OR; and the connection of (7) in the opposite direction, i.e. from the singular side of the OR to the plural side of the AND, contributes no connective information since the nature of the OR relationship is such that any impulse going into the plural side of an OR automatically goes on through to the next node as if the OR were not present; hence for nodes connecting to the plural side of the OR, identification of (a) connection to the OR node plus (b) connection to the AND node provides no further information than (b) alone provides.

A line which is not internal is EXTERNAL. An external line joins a node either to another node or to a zero element. In the former case it represents a two-way connection, a selection in both directions. That is, an external line connecting a node *n* to another node *m* represents two identifications of connections, (1) from *n* to *m,* (2) from *m* to *n;* and an external line from a node *n* to a zero element represents one identification of a connection, from *n* to Ø.

A combination of nodes connected to each other by internal lines, or a single node not connected by internal lines to another, together with the identifiers of connections to other such combinations, may be called a NECTION. These identifiers of connections to other nections may be called its TERMINALS. Thus each external line joining one nection to another represents two terminals. Some representative types of nections are shown in Figure 23; the terminals are diagrammed as lines.

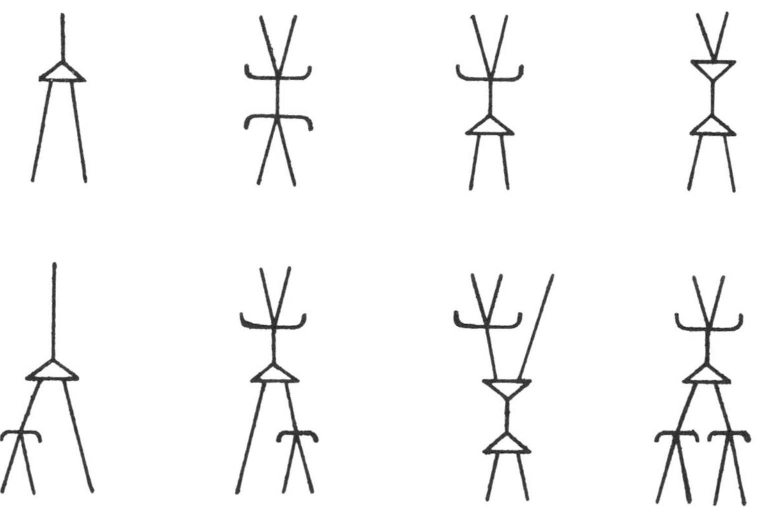

Figure 23.

For most purposes a satisfactory measure of surface information in a graph is provided by a count of the terminals. Consider again the graphs of Figure 21, repeated in Figure 24 with the terminals separately indicated. The graph at the right — i.e. that without the repetition — is simpler in that it has one less terminal.

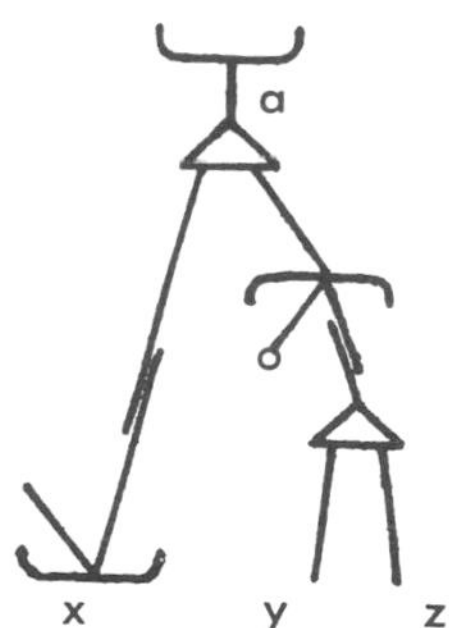

Figure 24.

Each terminal in a graph carries a certain amount of information. It represents a selection of a specific nection from the set of all nections to which it might attach. That set does not comprise all the nections in the language; rather, the general principles of organization of linguistic structure impose strict limitations upon what nections can be selected by a terminal at any position in the structure. For example a terminal on the downward side of an AND in a morphemic sign pattern connects to a morphon — so it represents a selection from a choice of some three or four dozen possibilities. The amount of information involved in specifying such a choice is considerably less than, say, that required to select a morpheme from the set of two or three thousand or so morphemes, or that which would be needed to select a nection if the range of choice included all of the many thousands of nections in a linguistic structure as a whole.

In most comparisons of alternative descriptions the varying amount of information represented by the terminals in different areas of linguistic structure can be ignored. But this simple measure is not sufficiently discriminating for certain situations, such as that shown in Figure 25. The two alternatives have the same number of terminals, but the graph at the right actually represents a more complicated description than that at the left under either of two conditions. First, if the information value of each terminal is the same as that of every other within each graph, as would presumably be the case if it is part of a tactic pattern, then the amount of information represented by each terminal in the graph at the right is slightly greater than that in the graph at the left, since that at the right has

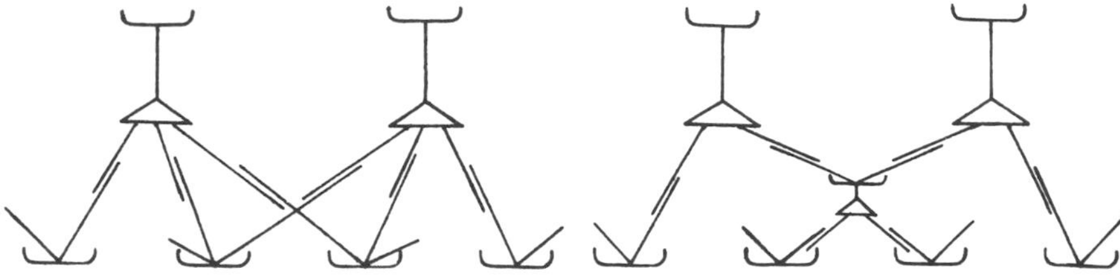

Figure 25.

more nections (i.e. one more) among which each terminal selects. On the other hand, if the diagram is taken as representing part of a sign pattern, say the morphemic sign pattern, then the terminals of the graph at the right have considerably more information than those at the left; for if the sign pattern is organized in the manner of the diagram at the left, then each terminal leading downward from a morphemic sign represents a choice among a very small number of possibilities; but if the type of organization shown at the right is allowed, the possibility would exist for hundreds of additional nections like that at the right to be present in the sign pattern, and the surface information value of every terminal leading down from a morphemic sign would be greatly increased. Therefore, for example, we refrain from identifying a common component *ar* in *car* and *art;* it would represent a spurious generalization. Moreover, the organization of a sign pattern according to the graph at the left is apparently to be arrived at as a matter of general linguistic theory rather than separately in the analysis of individual languages.

Of the numerous principles that have been put forth at various times to guide the conduct of linguistic analysis (e.g. in Nida 1949), some are invalid or superfluous because (1) they are based upon unsound theoretical foundations, or (2) they involve relatively aimless classifying without apparent theoretical justification, or (3) they were of use only in their roles as steps in unsuccessful procedures of analysis; others, however, are entirely or largely valid and remain useful. The validity of these latter does not rest upon their own inherent virtues nor on some other independent foundations; rather, they are derivable from the simplicity principle, as implemented through the concepts of surface information and effective information. This is true, for example, of the principles of biuniqueness and complementary distribution in phonology (cf. Lamb 1966b), and of several (but not all) of the criteria that have been put forth for determining immediate constituents (Wells 1947, Nida 1949:86-95).

The determination of the immediate constituents of sentences, phrases, and words is of course not important as an end in itself; rather, such determination is an approach to the description of the tactic pattern of a

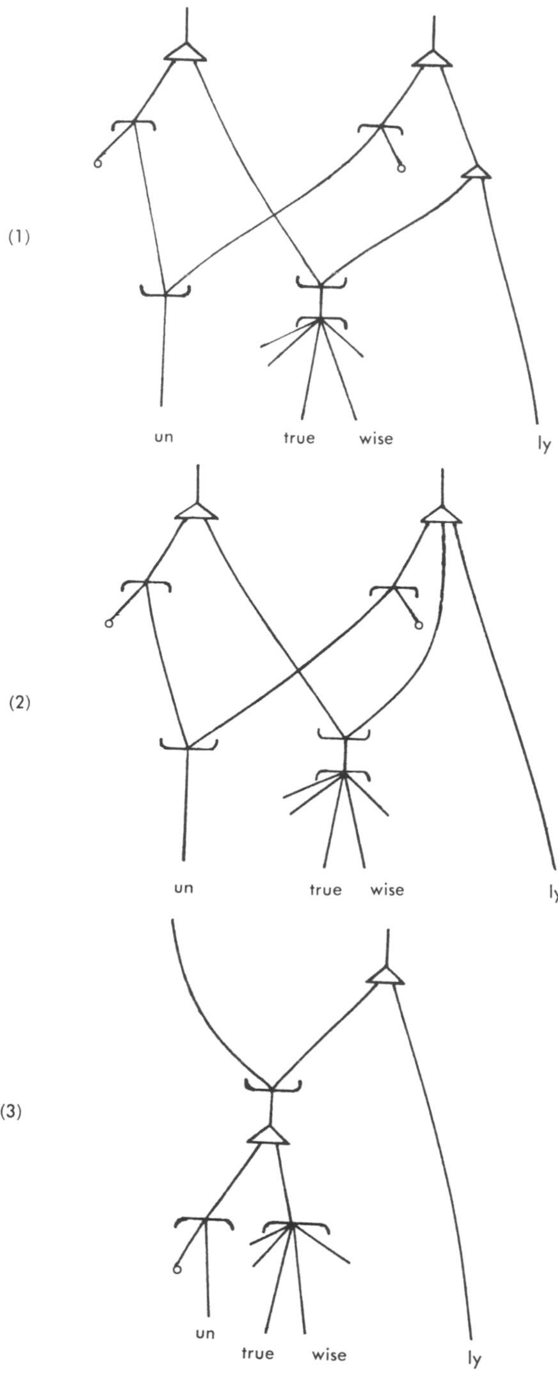

Figure 26.

stratal system (e.g. the lexotactics of some language). Every valid "cut" into immediate constituents represents a construction (i.e. a downward AND) in the tactic pattern. Alternative immediate constituent analyses mean alternatives in the tactic description; that alternative is to be preferred which is simpler. Consider, for example, the English word *untruly,* which offers these possibilities for analysis: (*un*)(*true ly*), (*un true*)(*ly*), (*un*)(*true*)(*ly*). The choice among the alternatives depends upon how they fit into the tactic description, which must of course account for other forms as well, in particular such forms as *truly* and *untrue,* and for the fact that the distribution of *true, untrue, wise, unwise,* etc., is different from that of *truly, untruly, wisely, unwisely,* etc. The three analyses are shown in Figure 26. Diagram (1), for the analysis (*un*)(*true ly*), has quite obvious excess surface information whose elimination results in diagram (2), representing the three-way cut. But (2) can be further simplified to (3). Thus the analysis (*un true*)(*ly*) fits the simplest tactic description, and is for that reason to be considered the correct immediate constituent analysis. This is also the analysis that would be arrived at by applying the principles of Wells or Nida.

Superficial Information

Two graphic descriptions may differ in effective information, in which case they also differ in surface information; or they may have the same effective information but different surface information; or they may have the same surface information, in which case they are also the same with

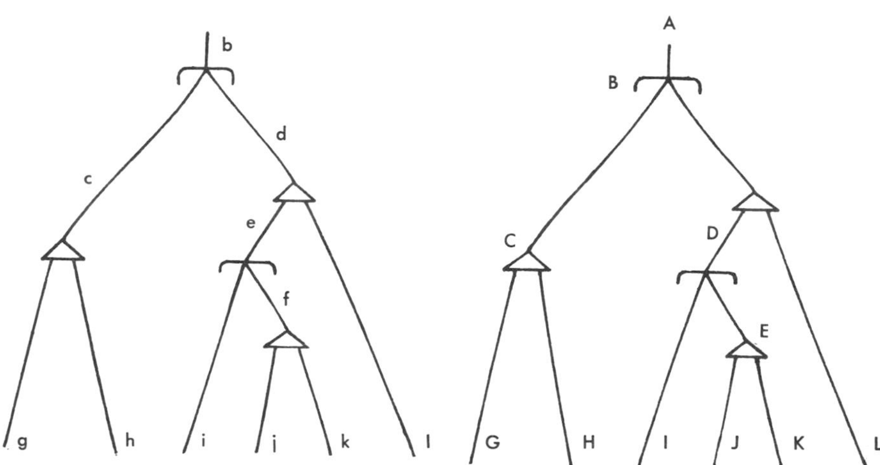

Figure 27.

respect to effective information. In the case of algebraic descriptions a further type of distinction is useful. Two algebraic descriptions may be said to differ in surface information if they describe different graphs, i.e. graphs which differ in surface information. But if two algebraic descriptions have the same surface information, they may nevertheless differ in SUPERFICIAL INFORMATION. For example, descriptions (1), (2), and (3) below differ in superficial information but have the same surface (and effective) information, since they are merely alternative descriptions of the same graph, shown in Figure 27. In the figure the same graph is shown twice with two different labellings; labels are for lines at the left, for nections at the right. Description (3), which uses the labelling at the right, has a NAME and a FORMULA for each nection, separated by the equals sign; the formula for a nection *N* specifies the nections to which the terminals of *N* attach.

(1) b / c,d
c / g h
d / e l
e / i,f
f / j k

(2) b / gh,(i,jk)l

(3) B = A / C,D.
C = B / G H
D = B / (I,E) L
E = D / J K

While the choice between descriptions differing in effective information or surface information is of considerable scientific significance, the comparison of descriptions which differ only in superficial information depends on esthetic and practical considerations, such as readability and the use to which the description is to be put. It is often desirable for an algebraic description to use more than the minimum number of symbols that would be necessary to uniquely specify a graphic description. Thus a description of the type exemplified by (3) is much better suited to the process of decoding texts than (1) and (2), while encoding is readily performed with descriptions of any of the three types (i.e., (3) is equally well suited to encoding and decoding).

In the description of diversification in an alternation pattern it will save trouble for the reader if an indication of the conditioning environments is given, even though such indication only repeats information already specified in the description of the associated tactic and knot patterns. Repetition of this type involves only superficial information, and is merely a means of coping with the inherent limitations of algebraic notation for representing linguistic structure. Thus the diversification for the English lexon ^{LN}/good/ depicted in Figure 7 could be described as

$$^{LN}\text{good} \;/\; ^{M}\text{beT} + {}^{M}\text{gud}$$

if ^{M}beT and ^{M}gud are used as symbols for the morphemes to which ^{LN}/good/ leads; and the conditions for the occurrence of the one realization or the other are specified in the tactics, to which the reader of the description may refer. The reader will be spared the trouble of referring to the tactics, however, if the formula for the diversification includes the relevant tactic information:

$$\begin{array}{rcl} ^{LN}\text{good} & \| & \text{—}(\text{er}_1,\text{est}) \;/\; ^{M}\text{beT} \\ + & \| & \text{—} \;/\; ^{M}\text{gud} \end{array}$$

A formula of this type may be called a REALIZATION RULE (cf. Lamb 1964a). It states that the structural relationships associated with ^{LN}/good/ are such that the realization ^{M}/beT/ occurs only when the comparative suffix or the superlative suffix follows; otherwise, i.e. in any other environment, the realization ^{M}/gud/ occurs.

Some Practical Considerations Concerning Description

Theoretically an entire stratal system could be described by a graph. And such a description is a practical possibility for a hypophonemic system or a (basic) phonemic system of a language, since for these two the number of lines and nodes is of quite manageable size. But for a morphemic, lexemic, or sememic system the graph would contain far too many lines and nodes to be practically feasible. Graphs of portions of these systems can enhance the clarity and readability of a description (as illustrated in the Appendix), but the description proper must take another form.

The following set of conventions provides some guides for the choice of symbols for use in algebraic or tabular descriptions as well as for labelling graphs.

Brackets consisting of slant lines and level identifiers may be used to distinguish structural levels. Symbols enclosed in such brackets stand for structural elements as follows:

^{H}/ . . . /	hypersememes
^{HS}/ . . . /	hypersememic signs
^{HN}/ . . . /	hypersemons
^{S}/ . . . /	sememes
^{SS}/ . . . /	sememic signs
^{SN}/ . . . /	semons
^{L}/ . . . /	lexemes
^{LS}/ . . . /	lexemic signs
^{LN}/ . . . /	lexons

^{M}/ . . . /	morphemes
^{MS}/ . . . /	morphemic signs
^{MN}/ . . . /	morphons
^{P}/ . . . /	(basic) phonemes
^{PS}/ . . . /	(basic) phonemic signs
^{PN}/ . . . /	(basic) phonons
^{H}/ . . . /	hypophonemes
^{HS}/ . . . /	hypophonemic signs

Although the brackets ^{H}/ . . . / and ^{HS}/ . . . / are in themselves ambiguous, their two uses, at the top and the bottom of linguistic structure, will ordinarily confine them to different contexts, and the symbols they enclose will be quite different, so that no confusion is likely to result.

Among other uses, these brackets (or, in suitable contexts, other level indicators) provide for economy in the use of symbols, since the same letter or sequence of letters can be used for elements at different levels. Thus ^{MN}/a/ for a given language designates a different unit from ^{P}/a/, as specified by the brackets. The letter "a" is thus allowed to serve a dual function, and this practice can also serve mnemonic purposes, in that ^{MN}/a/ may be used as the symbol for a morphon which has ^{P}/a/ as a realization (i.e. for a morphon which has a significant connection to ^{P}/a/).

The following symbols, chosen to have a mnemonic connection with their articulatory (i.e. primary) manifestations, may be used for hypophonemic signs, hypophonemes, and phonons (with levels distinguished by brackets, as indicated above):

Lb	Labial
Ap	Apical
Rz	Retracted (a component of English ^{PS}/r/, ^{PS}/z/, and ^{PS}/s/)
Fr	Frontal
Do	Dorsal
Pd	Postdorsal
Ph	Pharyngeal
Gl	Glottal
Cl	Closed (i.e. stop)
Sp	Spirant
Ns	Nasal
Uv	Unvoiced
Vo	Vocalic
Hi	High
Mi	Mid
Lo	Low

Phonemic signs, phonemes, and morphons may be symbolized by alphabetic characters, in keeping with the traditional conventions of classical phonemic writing.

A morphemic sign may be symbolized by the string of characters which symbolizes its morphonic realization, e.g., ^{MS}/gud/*good*. However, when a language has a standard orthography, as in the case of English, the ordinary orthography may be used instead, e.g., ^{MS}/good/, or the orthoggraphy may be used for the morpheme and/or the lexon while the morphonic writing is used for the morphemic sign. A morpheme may generally be symbolized by the symbol used for the morphemic sign to which it leads (except for the brackets). When two or more morphemes lead to the same morphemic sign, they may be distinguished from each other by numerical subscripts, e.g. ^{M}/$well_1$/, ^{M}/$well_2$/ (both of which lead down to ^{MS}/well/).

A lexon may be symbolized by the same symbol (except for the brackets) as is used for its morphemic realization. If a lexon has two or more morphemic realizations, one of them may be chosen, preferably the one which occurs in the greater variety of environments.

Similarly, the symbols for elements higher in the linguistic structure may be chosen on the basis of the symbols used for their realizations, in the manner indicated for the morphemic system. But any other combination of letters may be chosen if the readability or the esthetic or mnemonic quality of the description may be enchanced thereby: e.g., ^{SS}/past/, ^{SN}/pl/, ^{L}/Acc/. In the symbol for a lexemic sign or a lexeme, hyphen may be used to separate the symbols for the lexons of its lexonic realization, e.g. ^{LS}/under-stand/, ^{L}/wood-peck-er/. The same device may be used (mutatis mutandis) in the sememic system.

The description of a stratal system is probably most conveniently presented in two parts: the tactic description and the realizational description. The latter is the description of the realizational portion of the stratal system, i.e. the alternation pattern, the knot pattern, and the sign pattern; it may be called the DICTIONARY of the stratal system, e.g. the MORPHEMIC DICTIONARY, the LEXEMIC DICTIONARY. Alternatively, the lexemic dictionary may be called the LEXICON, the morphemic dictionary the MORPHICON, etc.

The dictionary of a stratal system may be organized as a list of entries, containing one entry for each sign of the system, together with a list of realization rules, containing one rule for each instance of diversification (i.e. each downward OR) in the alternation pattern. Each dictionary entry specifies the relationships which the sign has, downward to a combination of one or more ons and upward to the tactic pattern and to one or more ons of the next higher stratal system. The realization rules provide information leading from the top of the alternation pattern downward. As an alternative to a separate list of realization rules, the information pertaining to diversification may be incorporated among the dictionary entries for the signs of the system, as is done in the Appendix.

If the signs are symbolized by their onic realizations (according to the convention described above), then the symbol for a sign, which may serve as the heading of its dictionary entry, also functions as a specification of that realization. A sign which connects upward to a single eme has a simple dictionary entry, which need contain, besides the heading, only: (1) a VALENCE, i.e. an identification of the nection in the tactic pattern to which the eme directly connects, and (2) identification of the on or ons of the next higher system to which it connects. If the eme connects to only one on of the next higher system (i.e. if neutralization is not present), and if the convention is followed of symbolizing the on in the same way as its realization, then the further convention may be adopted of not repeating that symbol in the dictionary entry. In this case the simple dictionary entry consists only of (1) the heading, which identifies the sign, the eme, the upper on, and the lower ons which are downward components of the sign, and (2) the valence of the eme.

A typical dictionary will also have various types of complex entries, with complications corresponding to the different types of discrepancy that can be present in the realizational portion of a stratal system. Where a sign leads upward to more than one eme, because of neutralization in the knot pattern or portmanteau realization, a separate subentry may be given for each eme, with proper indication of the relationships involved. One set of conventions for treating these and other interstratal discrepancies is illustrated in the Appendix.

BIBLIOGRAPHY

BARKER, M. A. R.

1964 Klamath grammar. University of California Publications in Linguistics 32.

BILIGIRI, H. S.

1959 Kannada verb: Two models. Indian Linguistics 2:66-89.

BLOCH, BERNARD

1947 English verb inflection. Language 23:399-418; RIL 243-254.

1948 A set of postulates for phonemic analysis. Language 24:3-46.

1950 Studies in colloquial Japanese IV: Phonemics. Language 26:86-125; RIL 329-348.

CHOMSKY, NOAM

1957 Syntactic structures. The Hague, Mouton.

1964 Current issues in linguistic theory. The Hague, Mouton.

1965 Aspects of the theory of syntax. Cambridge, M. I. T. Press.

CONKLIN, HAROLD C.

1962 Lexicographical treatment of folk taxonomies. *In* F. W. Householder and S. Saporta (eds.), Problems in Lexicography. Indiana University Research Center in Anthropology, Folklore, and Linguistics, Publication 21.

1964 Ethnogenealogical method. *In* Ward H. Goodenough (ed.) Explorations in cultural anthropology: Essays in honor of George Peter Murdock. New York, McGraw-Hill.

FRAKE, CHARLES O.

1961 The diagnosis of disease among the Subanun of Mindanao. American Anthropologist 63:113-132.

GLEASON, H. A., Jr.

1964 The organization of language: A stratificational view. *In* Monograph Series on Languages and Linguistics, No. 17, Report on the 15th Annual R. T. M. on Linguistics and Language Studies, Georgetown University.

GOODENOUGH, WARD H.

1956 Componential analysis and the study of meaning. Language 32:195-216.

HALLE, MORRIS

1959 The sound pattern of Russian. The Hague, Mouton.

HALLIDAY, M. A. K.

1961 Categories of the theory of grammar. Word 17:241-292.

HAMMEL, E. A. (ed.)
1965 Formal semantic analysis. American Anthropologist 67, No. 5, Pt. 2.

HARRIS, ZELLIG S.
1942 Morpheme alternants in linguistic analysis. Language 18:169-180; RIL 109-115.
1951 Methods in structural linguistics. Chicago, University of Chicago Press.
1954 Distributional structure. Word 10:146-162.
1957 Cooccurrence and transformation in linguistic structure. Language 33:283-340.
1965 Transformational theory. Language 41:363-401.

HJELMSLEV, LOUIS
1943 Omkring sprogteoriens grundlaeggelse. Copenhagen. English translation by Francis J. Whitfield, Prolegomena to a theory of language. 2nd ed., Madison, University of Wisconsin Press, 1961.

HOCKETT, CHARLES F.
1942 A system of descriptive phonology. Language 18:3-21; RIL 97-108.
1947a Componential analysis of Sierra Popoluca. IJAL 13:258-267.
1947b Peiping phonology. JAOS 67:253-267; RIL 217-228.
1947c Problems of morphemic analysis. Language 23:321-343; RIL 229-242.
1954 Two models of grammatical description. Word 10:210-231; RIL 386-399.
1955 A manual of phonology. IJAL Memoir 11.
1961 Linguistic elements and their relations. Language 37:29-53.

LAMB, SYDNEY M.
1961 MT research at the University of California, Berkeley. *In* H. P. Edmundson (ed.), Proceedings of the National Symposium on Machine Translation, Englewood Cliffs, Prentice-Hall.
1962a Outline of stratificational grammar. Berkeley, ASUC.
1962b On the mechanization of syntactic analysis. *In* 1961 International Conference on Machine Translation of Languages and Applied Language Analysis, London, Her Majesty's Stationery Office.
1964a On alternation, transformation, realization, and stratification. *In* Monograph Series on Languages and Linguistics, No. 17, Report of the 15th Annual R. T. M. on Linguistics and Language Studies, Georgetown University.

1964b The sememic approach to structural semantics. *In* A. Kimball Romney and Roy Goodwin D'Andrade (eds.), Transcultural Studies in Cognition. American Anthropologist 66, No. 3, Pt. 2:57-78.

1965a The nature of the machine translation problem. Journal of Verbal Learning and Verbal Behavior 4:196-210.

1965b Kinship terminology and linguistic structure. *In* E. A. Hammel (ed.), Formal semantic analysis. American Anthropologist 67, No. 5, Pt. 2:37-64.

1966a Epilegomena to a theory of language. Romance Philology 19:531-573.

1966b Prolegomena to a theory of phonology. Language 42:536-573.

1966c The use of semantic information for the resolution of syntactic ambiguity. *In* Actes du Colloque International de Linguistique Appliquée, Faculté des Lettres et des Sciences Humaines, Nancy.

1966d Linguistic structure and the production and decoding of discourse. *In* Victor E. Hall (ed.), Speech, Language, and Communication, UCLA Forum in Medical Sciences. Berkeley and Los Angeles, University of California Press.

In press Stratificational linguistics as a basis for machine translation. *In* Bulcsu Laszlo (ed.), Approaches to Language Data Processing. The Hague, Mouton.

LOUNSBURY, FLOYD G.

1956 A semantic analysis of the Pawnee kinship usage. Language 32:158-194.

1964a The structural analysis of kinship semantics. Proceedings of the Ninth International Congress of Linguists. The Hague, Mouton.

1964b A formal account of the Crow- and Omaha-type kinship terminologies. *In* Ward H. Goodenough (ed.), Explorations in Cultural Anthropology; Essays in honor of George Peter Murdock. New York, McGraw-Hill.

1965 Another view of the Trobriand kinship categories. *In* E. A. Hammel (ed.), Formal semantic analysis. American Anthropologist 67, No. 5, Pt. 2:142-185.

NIDA, EUGENE A.

1948 The identification of morphemes. Language 24:414-441.

1949 Morphology, the descriptive analysis of words. Ann Arbor, University of Michigan Press.

NOREEN, A.
1903-18 Vårt Språk (Lund). Selections translated into German by H. W. Pollak, Einführung in die wissenschaftliche Betrachtung der Sprache. Halle, 1923.

PITTMAN, RICHARD S.
1948 Nuclear structures in linguistics. Language 24:287-292; RIL 275-278.

SHAUMJAN, S. K.
1965 Outline of the applicational generative model for the description of language. Foundations of Language 1:189-222.

SHIPLEY, WILLIAM F.
1964 Maidu grammar. University of California Publications in Linguistics 41.

SWADESH, MORRIS
1934 The phonemic principle. Language 10:117-129; RIL 32-37.

TRAGER, GEORGE L.
1955 French morphology: Verb inflection. Language 31:511-529.

TRUBETZKOY, N. S.
1939 Grundzüge der phonologie. TCLP 7.

TWADDELL, W. FREEMAN
1935 On defining the phoneme. Language Monograph No. 16; RIL 55-80.

WALLACE, ANTHONY F. C., and JOHN ATKINS
1960 The meaning of kinship terms. American Anthropologist 62:58-80.

WELLS, RULON S.
1947 Immediate constituents. Language 23.81-117; RIL 186-207.
1949 Automatic alternation. Language 25:99-116.

EXERCISES

1. Maidu

1.	wépa	'(the) coyote'	wépa na	'toward (the) coyote'
2.	páno	'(the) grizzly'	páno na	'toward (the) grizzly'
3.	hemé	'(the) gopher'	hemé na	'toward (the) gopher'
4.	kojó	'(the) valley'	kojó na	'toward (the) valley'
5.	kylé	'(the) woman'	kylé na	'toward (the) woman'
6.	p̓ýbe	'(the) boy'	p̓ýbe na	'toward (the) boy'

   a. These data give evidence of two distribution classes (or valence classes) in Maidu morphotactics. Call them "Class A" and "Class B." What are the members of each?

   b. Give a graphic and an algebraic description of that portion of the morphemic system of Maidu for which these data furnish evidence.

   c. Given /hybó/ 'house' what is the probable meaning of /hybóna/?

   d. Given /kulúna/ 'twilight' can a meaning be determined for /kulú/?

2. This is part of the morphemic system of a very simple artificial language. Assume that every combination of morphemes allowed by the morphotactics is possible.

   a. What is the longest string of morphons generated by this system? What is the shortest?

   b. Assign each of the following strings to one of these three categories: ill-formed, ambiguous, or well-formed and non-ambiguous. (a) daku, (b), mikkada, (c) kakami, (d) kamika, (e) kamiku, (f) mikadi

   c. How many strings of morphemes does the system generate? Is the number of strings of morphons the same or not? Explain your answer.

   d. State a general procedure for determining how many combinations a tactic pattern generates (provided the number is finite), without actually generating combinations and counting.

3. How many combinations of phonemes are generated by the phonotactics of Figure 5?

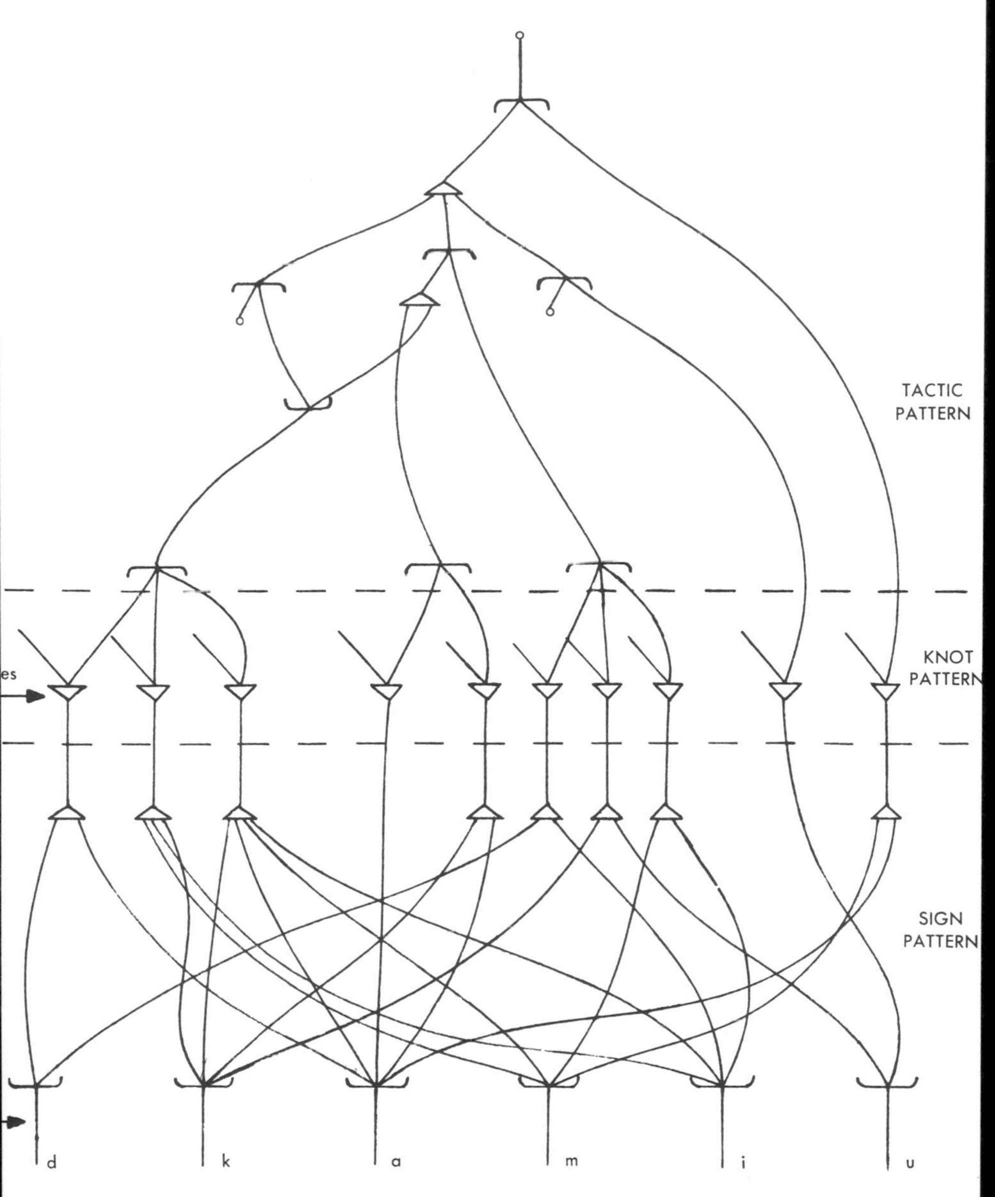

Exercise 2

4. Latin

The following forms are written in a classical phonemic transcriptio (i.e. each character represents a combination of one or more hypo phonemes). Account for the phonological alternation and list th morphemes.

NOMINATIVE	GENITIVE	
rēks	rēgis	'king'
duks	dukis	'leader'
arks	arkis	'citadel'
ops	opis	'power'
plēps	plēbis	'the people'
urps	urbis	'the city'

5. Latin

The following forms are written in traditional Latin orthography which serves as an accurate classical phonemic representation of these forms. (The letter c represents a voiceless velar stop.) Account fo the phonological alternation and list the morphemes.

NOM.	GEN.	GLOSS	NOM.	GEN.	GLOSS
fel	fellis	bile	mel	mellis	honey
cor	cordis	heart	lac	lactis	milk
os	ossis	bone	far	farris	sp. grai
glīs	glīris	dormouse	os	ōris	mouth
mōs	mōris	custom	flōs	flōris	flower
crūs	crūris	leg	mūs	mūris	mouse
aes	aeris	copper	mās	māris	male
cinis	cineris	ashes	pulvis	pulveris	dust
vōmis	vōmeris	plowshare	tempus	temporis	time
corpus	corporis	body	lepus	leporis	charm
tellūs	tellūris	earth	pīgnus	pīgnoris	pledge
vēr	vēris	spring	fūr	fūris	thief
ūber	ūberis	udder	verber	verberis	whip
mulier	mulieris	woman	ebur	eboris	ivory
femur	femoris	thigh	rōbur	rōboris	oak
marmor	marmoris	marble	murmur	murmuris	murmur
vultur	vulturis	vulture	fulgur	fulguris	lightnin
calcar	calcāris	spur	soror	sorōris	sister
honor	honōris	honor	amor	amōris	love

Additional material:

prōdīs	you go forth	prōdis	you publish, report
prōdit	he goes forth	prōdit	he publishes, reports
vincīs	you bind, fasten	vincis	you conquer
vincit	he binds, fastens	vincit	he conquers

6. Natchez
   Account for the phonological alternation exhibited by the following data.

'one to ____'	'several to ____'	GLOSS
ˀayho·ˀis	ˀayi·ho·ˀis	think
tu·ho·ˀis	tuhuho·ˀis	beat
pi·Lhalˀis	pi·lihalˀis	plaster
kihelu·ˀis	ki·helu·ˀis	tie
paYheLsu·ˀis	payaheLsu·ˀis	stand on
hemhalˀis	hemi·halˀis	destroy
polohalˀis	polo·halˀis	lathe
toMhalˀis	tomohalˀis	lend
tolhalˀis	toli·halˀis	twist
kawhelku·s	kawi·helku·s	dip
we·Lhaki·s	we·lehaki·s	talk
wanhetahnu·ˀis	wani·hetahnu·ˀis	quarrel
puLchaLsi·s	pulcuhaLsi·s	write
wacho·ˀis	wacaho·ˀis	scatter
pi·ho·ˀis	pihiho·ˀis	whip
pataheNci·s	pata·heNci·s	put together
ti·Mhaki·s	ti·mihaki·s	get drunk
tuku·hesku·s	tukuhuhesku·s	rub
mehalˀis	me·halˀis	extinguish
tisa·hekti·s	tisahahekti·s	sneeze
peyhohsi·s	peyi·hohsi·s	store

7. Show that the graphs in each of the sets of Figure 17 convey the same effective information.

8. Draw the diagram of the simplest possible capotactics which will generate all and only the following combinations of capemes (a capeme is any of the following: A, B, C, D, E, F, G):

A
A B C
A B D E
A B D F
A B D G

9. Simplify this diagram:

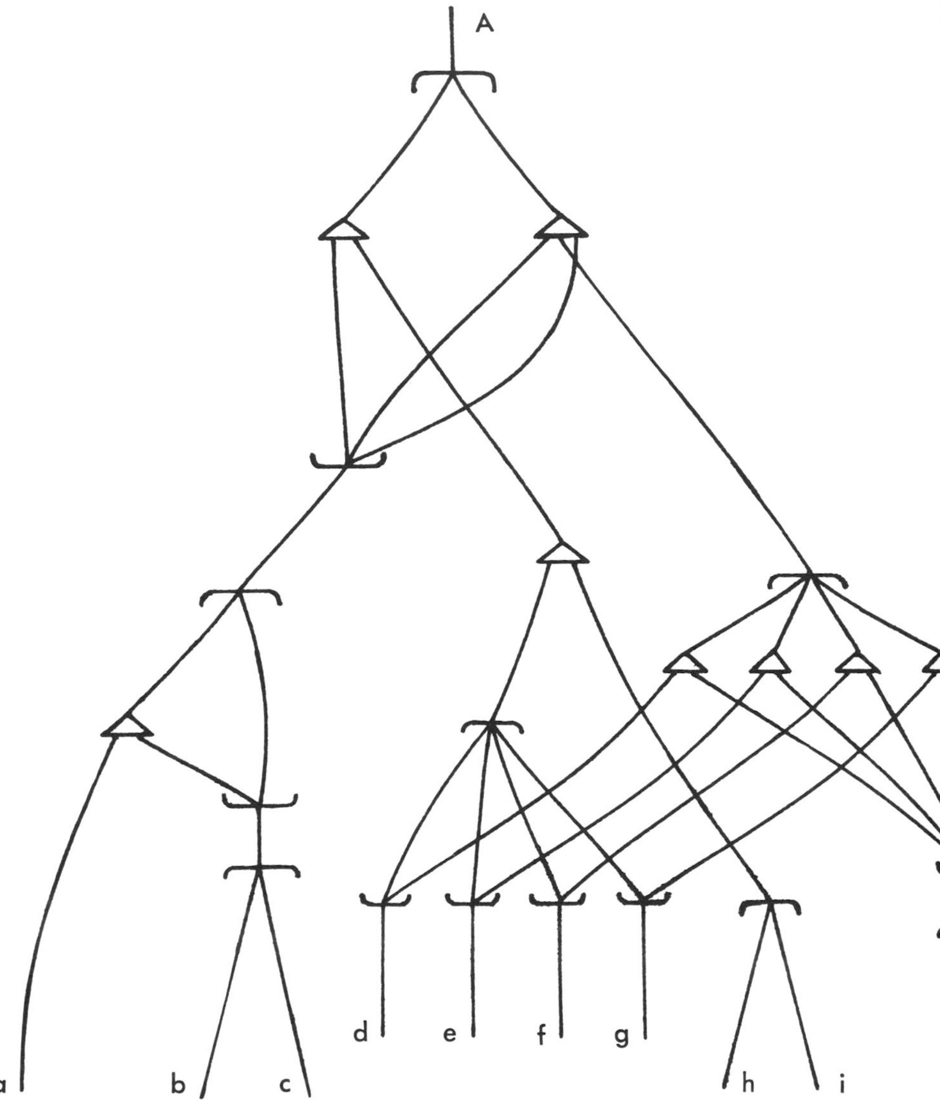

Exercise 9

10. Simplify this diagram:

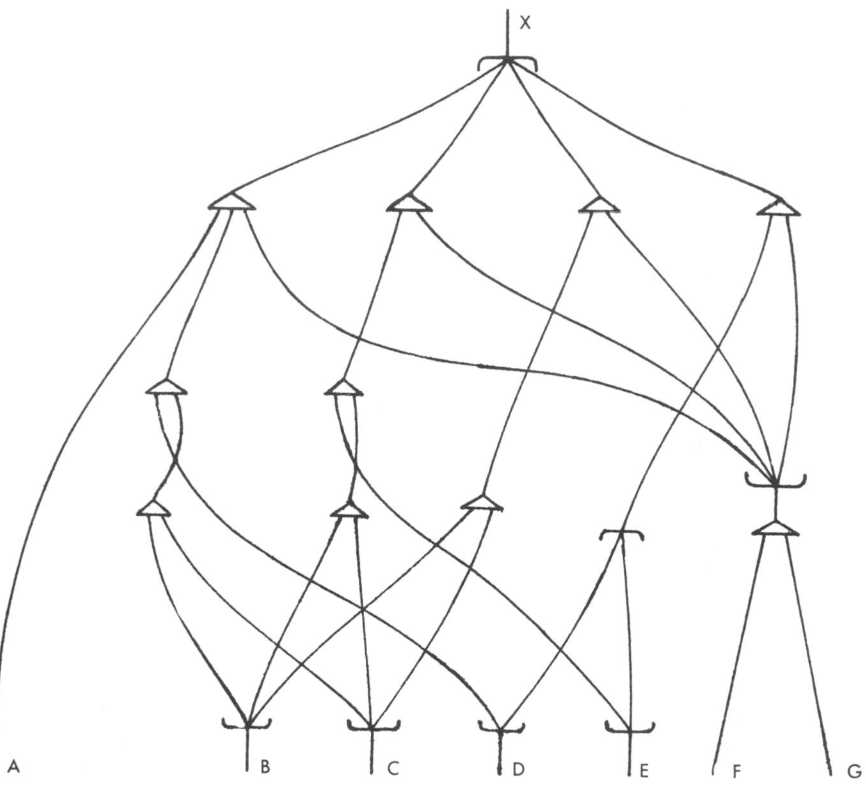

Exercise 10

11. Draw the diagram of the simplest possible capotactics which will generate all and only the following combinations of capemes:

A C	B D	D
A D	B E	D F J
A E	B G J	E
A G J	B H J	E F J
A H J	C	I J
B C	C F J	

12. English

Considering each of the following sets separately, make a decision as to whether the forms should be regarded as representing single morphemes or combinations of morphemes. Add appropriate additional forms to any set if you find it helpful to do so. What are the appropriate considerations in arriving at a decision? Give reasons for each decision.

Set A:

cranberry	strawberry
raspberry	barberry
huckleberry	elderberry

Set B:

mushroom	crawdad	lobster

Set C:

otter	badger
tiger	gopher
beaver	fisher

Set D:

patter	spatter	scatter
clatter	shatter	splatter
tatter	batter	chatter

Set E:

gleam	glow	glimmer	glisten
glare	glance	gleed	glint
glitter	gloaming	gloze	glimpse

Set F:

slip	slop	slide	slash	slurp	slime	slush
flip	flop	glide	bash	burp	grime	mush
drip	drop	ride	dash	urp		
trip		stride	crash			
			smash			

Set G:

confer	confuse	conform	confine	contain	conceive	conduce
refer	refuse	reform	refine	retain	receive	reduce
infer	infuse	inform				induce
	perfuse	perform		pertain	perceive	
defer		deform	define	detain	deceive	deduce

APPENDIX

STRATIFICATIONAL ANALYSIS OF AN ENGLISH TEXT

by

Leonard E. Newell

I. INTRODUCTION

This appendix is an analysis on the lexemic and morphemic strata of an English text using as a model the stratificational theory as developed by Sydney M. Lamb.[1] Because of the preliminary nature of this treatment, no claims are made as to accuracy or exhaustiveness of the description. The presentation is to be regarded as highly tentative and is intended only to provide an example of the use of the theory in the description of a text.

The text is a portion of a tape recorded dinner conversation from which about 350 words of running text were selected. Two adults and two children participated in the conversation. M: indicates utterances by Mother, G: utterances by twelve-year-old son, F: utterances by Father and K: utterances by ten-year-old daughter.

The text is presented below in conventional orthography. In section 2.1 it is rewritten as strings of lexemes within sentences and in section 3.1 as strings of morphemes within words.

TEXT

M: What did you do at school this afternoon, Gordy?
G: Played baseball.
M: Played baseball? Did you make any hits?
G: No, no.
M: You didn't hit it?
G: I got to hit it once.
F: Did you get to first base?
G: Nope.
F: How come?
G: I struck out.
F: Struck out?
G: Second base to first and I was out.
F: Yea, but you didn't strike out then. They put you out on first.
G: I hit the ball to second base then he threw it to first and I was out.
F: Yea, if you strike out that means that there were three throws and you didn't hit any of them.
G: What do you call the other thing?
F: You were put out on first base.
M: What else did you do in school?
G: We had Lassie.
M: What's that about?
G: About a dog.
M: Yea, but what did you have to do?
G: I have something to do in that tonight for homework.
M: What did you do Kathy?

K: Well, we were writing stories about the movie we had yesterday or the day before yesterday about that Harriet Tubman. And then we drew pictures and then he said they were going to show the pictures to other schools to see if they would like to have the movie of Harriet Tubman . . . the class of that Mister Donello . . . he's the man that was helping the school . . . that showed us the pictures, and then the bell rang.

F: Hmh?

K: Then the bell rang and we had to go.

G: Today we had a . . . the fire alarm went.

K: Oh yea.

G: And it scared me so much that I jumped about six feet off the ground and everyone was scared and jumped up and started running out the door.

F: Did you all go outside?

G: Mhm.

M: Did you go down a chute?

G: Down a fire escape.

M: Just down the steps?

G: Mhm.

M: Not a chute huh?

G: U' 'u.

M: A slide? Do they have a slide there?

G: M' 'm.

M: They don't have any slide, huh? You know some schools have a great big tube and you just slide down and you get down faster.

G: We have to walk down.

F: You couldn't run, huh?

G: No! We'd be hanged at the break of day!

2. LEXEMIC SYSTEM

The lexemic description includes a sketch of the lexemic tactic pattern for all the well-formed sentences. Some utterances, considered not to be well formed, were excluded from the description as, for example, "Today we had a . . . the fire alarm went." The lexotactic pattern, however, accounts for the sentence "Today we had a fire drill" and "Today the fire alarm went." Minor sentence types illustrated by the utterances "Played baseball" or "About a dog" are not accounted for.

2.1 Lexemic Transcription Of The Text.

In the lexemic transcription lexemes are separated by spaces and the lexons of a lexeme are separated by hyphens. (The morphemic realization of some of these are discontinuous as specified by the morphotactic pattern, e.g., *have-en.*) The lexemic transcription indicates the ordering of lexemes as specified by the lexotactics. For some lexemes (e.g., *-ed*) the sequence of occurrence specified by the lexotactic pattern is adjusted by the morphotactics.[2]

M: What -m_2 -re -ed Q you do $this_2$ after-noon, Gordy?
G: -ed play base-ball -m_2.
M: -ed play base-ball -m_2? -re -ed Q you make any -s hit -s m_2?
G: No, no.
M: You -re -ed not hit it -m_2?
G: I -m_1 -ed get to hit it -m_2 one -ce.
F: -re -ed Q you get to_1 one-th-base -m_2?
G: Nope.
F: How-come?
G: I -m_1 -ed strike out.
F: -ed strike out?
G: Two-th-base -m_2 to_1 one-th and I -m_1 -ed be out.
F: Yea, but you -re -ed not strike out then, they -re -ed put you -m_2 out on one-th -m_2.
G: I -m_1 -ed hit the ball -m_2 to_1 two-th-base -m_2 then he -z_1 -ed throw it -m_2 to_1 one-th -m_2 and I -m_1 -ed be out.
F: Yea, if you -re strike out $that_4$ -z_1 mean $that_3$ $there_1$ -re -ed be three throw -s and you -re -ed not hit any -m_2 of they -m_2.
G: $What_1$ -m_2 -re Q you call the other thing -m_2?
F: You -re -ed be-en put out on one-th-base -m_2.
M: $What_1$ -m_2 else -re -ed Q you do in school -m_2?
G: We -re -ed have Lassie -m_2.
M: $What_1$ -m_2 -z_1 Q $that_4$ be about?
G: About a dog -m_2.
M: Yea, but $what_1$ -m_2 -re -ed you have to do?
G: I -m_1 have some-thing -m_2 to_2 do in $that_4$ -m_2 to-night for home-work -m_2.
M: $What_1$ -re -ed Q you do Kathy?
K: Well, we -re -ed be-ing write a -s story -s -m_2 about the movie we -ed have yester-day or the day be-fore yester-day -m_2 about $that_1$ Harriet Tubman -m_2, and then we -re -ed draw a -s picture -s -m_2, and then he -z_1 -ed say they -re -ed be-go-ing-to show the -s picture -s -m_2 to_1 other school -s -m_2 to-see-if they -re will -ould like to_2 have the movie -m_2 of Harriet Tubman -m_2 . . . the class of $that_1$ Mister Donello -m_2 . . . he -z_1 be the man $that_2$ -z_1 -ed be-ing help the school -m_2 . . . $that_2$ -z_1 -ed show we -m_2 the -s picture -s -m_2, and $then_1$ the bell -z_1 -ed ring.
F: Hmh?
K: $Then_1$ the bell -z_1 -ed ring and we -re -ed have to go.

G: To-day we -re -ed have a . . . the fire-alarm -z_1 -ed go.
K: Oh yea!
G: And it -z_1 -ed scare I -m_2 so-much-that I -m_1 -ed jump about six foot -s -m_2 off the ground -m_2 and every-one -z_1 -ed be-en scare and -z_1 -ed jump up and -z_1 -ed start run -ing -m_2 out the door -m_2.
F: -re -ed Q you all go out-side?
G: Mhm.
M: -re -ed Q you go down a chute -m_2?
G: Down a fire-escape -m_2.
M: Just down the -s step -s -m_2?
G: Mhm.
M: Not a chute -m_2 huh?
G: U' 'u.
M: A slide -m_2? -re Q they have a slide -m_2 there?
G: M' 'm.
M: They -re not have any slide -m_2 huh? You -re know some -s school -s have a great big tube -m_2 and you -re just slide down and you -re get down fast-er.
G: We -re have to walk down.
F: You -re can -ould not run huh?
G: No, we -re will -ould be-en hang at the break -m_2 of day -m_2.

2.2 Lexemic Tactic Pattern.

Sentence:
S / (MajSn,ExclSn,Itj) Inton

A sentence consists of one of three sentence types plus intonation. Of these, one is a major sentence type and is the only one of the three patterns containing a subject and a predicate. This preliminary presentation does not include a description of the intonation contours. (Word juncture and some features of stress and pitch would be accounted for in a more complete description of the morphemic system than is given here.) The form *huh,* closely associated with intonation, is not included in this description.

Major Sentence:
MajSn / [Conj] [how-come] Sn
Conj / and,but,or
'Yes but you didn't strike out then.'

Sentence:
Sn / [AttP] [SubClause] [Int] Clause [com Voc]

Attributive Phrase:
An attributive phrase may optionally occur as a modifier of any one of three constructions within the lexemic tactic pattern: it may occur as the

first constituent of a sentence in an adverbial function, as a modifier of a verb phrase (see below under *Verb Phrase*) or as a post-noun modifier (see below under *Noun Phrase*).

AttP / $AttP_1$ [AttP]

An attributive phrase consists of an *attributive phrase*$_1$ followed by an optional *attributive phrase.* This indicates the optional addition of attributive phrases to other attributive phrases or sequences of such.

'Today at school the fire-alarm went.'

$AttP_1$ / PrepP,InfP,LocP,TempP

An *attributive phrase*$_1$ consists of either a prepositional phrase, an infinitive phrase, a locative phrase or a temporal phrase.

Prepositional Phrase:

PrepP / Prep Obj

Prep / at,$about_2$,before,down,for,from,in,off,on,out,outside,to_1,up

Object:

Obj / Nom $-m_2$

An object consists of a nominal and an object marker $-m_2$. *Nominal* is discussed below under *Nominal.* The object marker is specified by the lexonic alternation pattern as $-m_2 + \emptyset$. $^{LN}/-m_2/$ is realized as zero when the nominal is other than the pronouns *he, I, she, they, we* or *who,* as specified by the morphotactics.

'At school the boys played ball.'

Infinitive Phrase:

InfP / to_2 VP

Verb phrases are described below under *Verb Phrase.*

'To get out of the school we had to run down the steps.'

Locative Phrase:

LocP / $outside_2$,$there_2$

'Outside the boys were playing ball.'

Temporal Phrase:

TempP / then,today,tonight,yesterday,NP

'Today the fire alarm went.'

A noun phrase occurs as a temporal phrase in sentences such as the following:

'The day before yesterday the fire alarm went.'

Subordinate Clause:

SubClause / (if, . . .) Clause

Interrogative:

Int / [RIP_1] (SubjDel $+ \emptyset$)

Interrogative consists of an optional relative interrogative pronoun and either a subject delay or zero in an ordered OR (see Figure 3). Zero is chosen if one of the interrogative pronouns occurs as subject of the clause or in the subject phrase, since interrogative pronouns cannot be delayed, because of the upward unordered ANDs labeled *IntDet, RelPr*$_1$ and *RelPr*$_2$. Delay of the subject is discussed in a description of the predicate under the heading *Subject Delay. Relative interrogative pronoun*$_1$ is discussed below under the heading *Relative Interrogative Pronoun.*

Clause:
Clause / Subj *(Conj)Pred
Clause [SubjDel] / Subj / Nom

Subject leads up to *clause* and an optional subject delay and down to *nominal.* Subject delay involves the formation of interrogative clauses as described below under the heading *Subject Delay.*

Nominal:
Nom / NPers,Pr,NP, RelPr$_1$,RelPr$_2$,RelPr$_3$

Personal Noun:
NPers / [DemDet] [Mister] NPers$_1$
DemDet / that$_1$, this$_2$
NPers$_1$ / NPers$_2$ [NPers$_1$]
NPers$_2$ / Donello,Gordy,Harriett,Kathy,Tubman, . . .
'the class of that Mister Donello'

The specification of *NPers*$_1$ and *NPers*$_2$ indicates that *NPers*$_2$ may be repeated, thus allowing sequences of personal nouns.
'the movie of Harriet Tubman'

Pronouns:
Pr / PrPers,PrDem,PrImp
PrPers / I,you$_1$,he,she,(they,we,you$_2$)[all]
'I got to hit it once.'
PrDem / that$_2$,this$_1$
'that$_2$ means that there were three throws'
PrImp / everyone,it,something,there$_1$
'everyone was scared'

Noun Phrase:
NP / [D] [NumOrd] [other] [Adj$_1$] [Adj$_2$] *(and,or)N [PostNMod] [Rel]

Determiner:
D / PosNom,Det$_1$, [about] Num

Possessive Nominal:
PosNom / Nom -'s
'Harriet Tubman's movie'

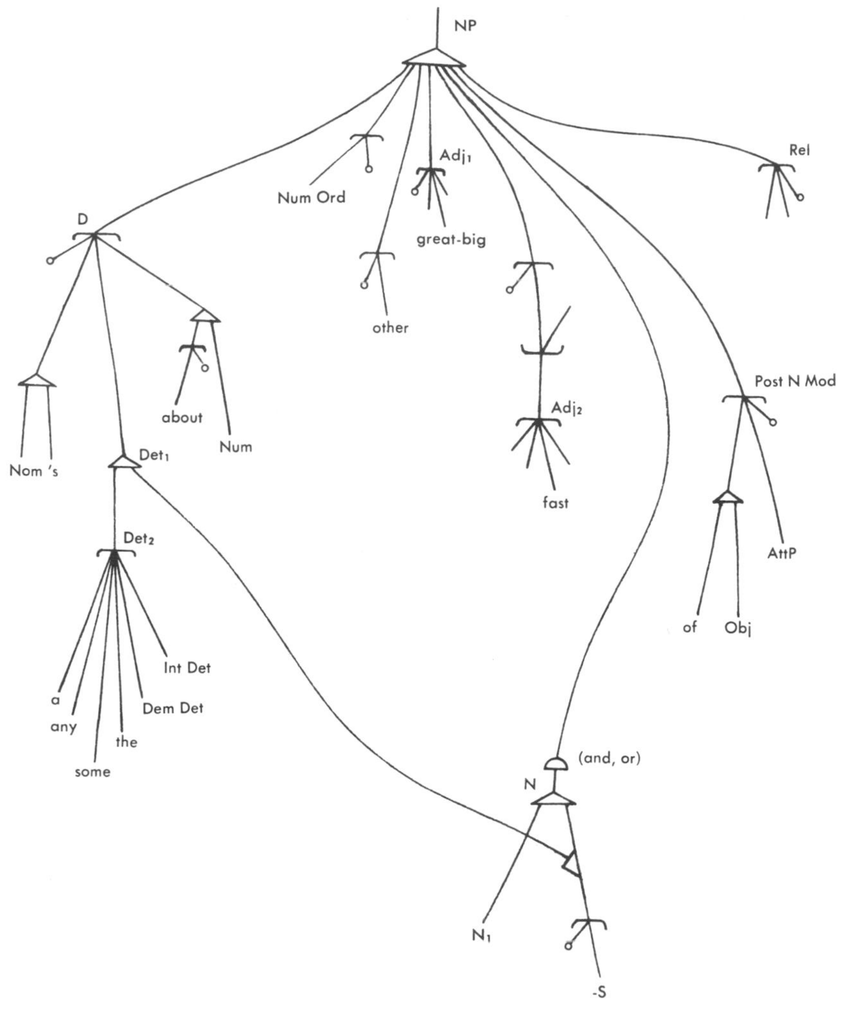

Figure 1

Determiner$_1$:

Det$_1$ / Det$_2$ =Nmb

Det$_2$ / a,any,some,the,DemDet,IntDet

Nmb / [-s]

Determiner$_1$ consists of a *determiner*$_2$ and a line going to a reduplication ode attached to *Nmb* (see below under *Noun*). This specifies number greement between determiner and noun.

'Did you make any hits?'

or a description of plural determiners and plural nouns see *Morphemic actic Pattern* (sec. 3.2).

IntDet indicates an upward unordered AND involving the relative interrogative pronouns *what*$_2$ and *which*$_2$ (see Figure 2 below). *Interrogative determiner* is described below under the heading *Relative Interrogative Pronoun.*

Numeral:

Num / one,two,three, . . .
NumOrd / Num -th

'I jumped about six feet off the ground'

Adjective$_1$:

Adj$_1$ / great-big, . . .

'some schools have a great big tube'

Adjective$_2$:

Adj$_2$ / fast, . . .

Noun:

N / (B,N$_1$) Nmb
B / ball,base,bell,break,call,class,do,dog,draw,foot,get,go,ground, hang,help,hit,jump,like,make,man,picture,play,ring,run,say, scare,school,score,see,show,side,slide,start,step,story,strike, throw,tube,walk,work
N$_1$ / afternoon,any,baseball,chute,day,door,fire-alarm,fire-escape, first-base,homework,movie,once,running,second

Bases (*B*) occur both as nouns as specified here and as verbs (see *Verb Phrase*).

Post-Noun Modifier:

PostNMod / AttP,of Obj

A post-noun modifier may be realized as either an attributive phrase or as *of* followed by an object.

'the class of that Mister Donello'

Relative:

Rel / (RelPr$_2$,RelPr$_3$) Clause

Relative is a post-noun modifier consisting of either *who, which*$_1$ or *that*$_{3a}$ followed by a clause in which the relative pronoun functions as a nominal.

Relative Interrogative Pronoun:

RIP$_1$ · Det$_2$ / IntDet / what$_2$,which$_2$

'What time did the bell ring?'
'Which boy hit the ball?'

RIP$_1$ / IntDet,RIP$_2$
RIP$_2$ / (RelPr$_1$,RelPr$_2$) else
(RIP$_2$,Rel) • Nom / RelPr$_2$ / who

'Who else did you see at school?'

'He was the man who rang the fire alarm.'

Nom · RIP_2 / $RelPr_1$ / $what_1$

'What else did you do in school?'

Rel · Nom / $RelPr_3$ / [which,$that_{3a}$]

'He's the man who was helping the school.'

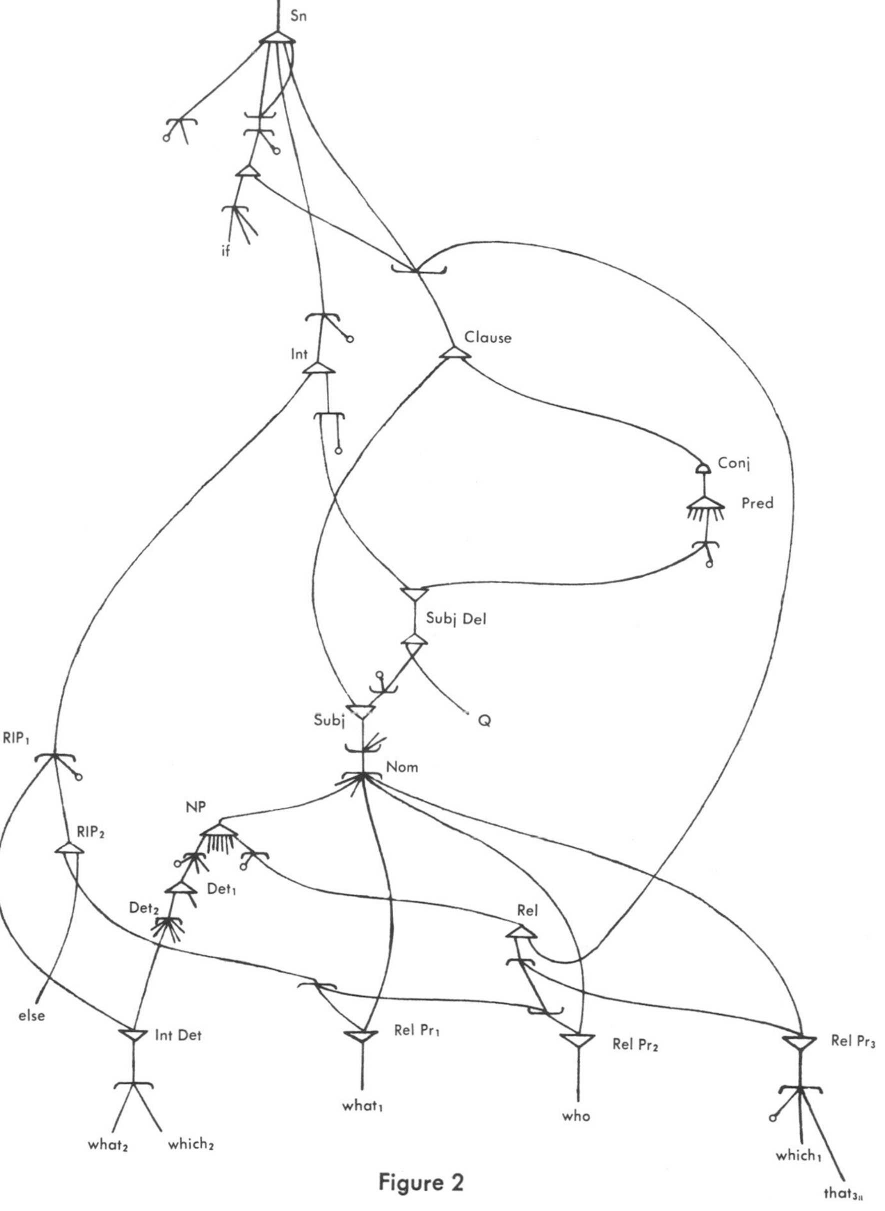

Figure 2

Nominal and *relative* optionally lead to a zero pronoun. In the example below, there is a zero relative pronoun following the word *movie*.

'We were writing stories about the movie we had yesterday.'

Predicate:

Pred / Con [Aux] [not] [SubjDel] [just] VP

Concord:

Con / $-m_1$,-re,$-z_1$

$-m_1$ indicates concord with a first person singular subject, $-z_1$ with a third person singular subject and *-re* with either a first person plural, a second person or a third person plural subject. For a discussion of the realization of the three concord elements at the morphemic stratum, see

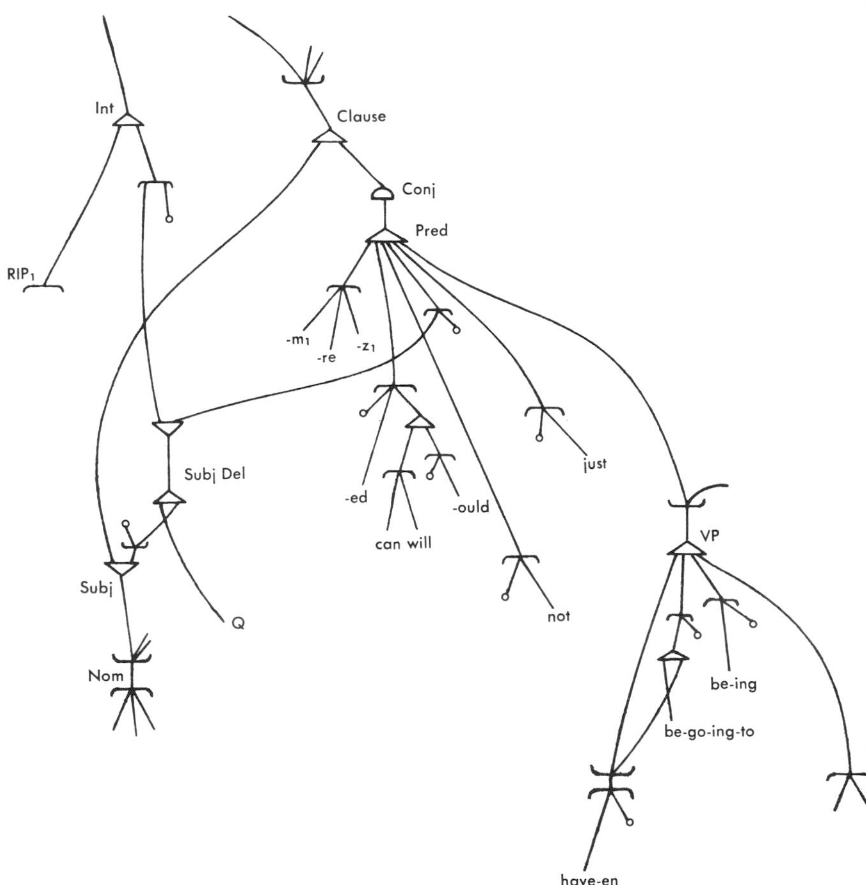

Figure 3

sec. 3.2 under the headings *Auxiliary* and *Verb,* and sec. 3.3 where portmanteaus involving concord elements are discussed.

Auxiliary:

Aux / -ed,(can,will) [-ould]

Auxiliary consists of either a past tense lexeme *-ed,* or *can* or *will* with an optional subjunctive lexeme *-ould.* The order of occurrence of the suffix *-ed* within a word is specified by the morphemic tactic pattern.

Subject Delay:

Int Pred / SubjDel / Q Subj

Q is a lexeme which is specified in the lexonic alternation pattern as follows: Q / do_1 + Ø. do_1 is the realization of ^{LN}Q if the morphotactic word auxiliary (*can, will,* etc.), constituents *have* or *be* of lexemes *have-en, be-go-ing-to* or *be-ing,* the constituent *be* of *be-en* (first constituent of a passive verb phrase), or linking verb *be.* If any of these latter are activated, ^{LN}Q is realized as zero.

In the formation of an interrogative clause, the following is indicated: an optional relative interrogative pronoun followed by the first line of an upward AND labeled *Subject Delay.* Here the impulse is delayed until activation of the second line from the predicate (at which time the subject is realized). The first line of an upward ordered AND labeled *Subject* is next and is delayed until the activation of the second line (SubjDel). One of three concord elements occurs next followed optionally by either *-ed, can* with an optional subjunctive or by *will* with an optional subjunctive. An optional *not* follows. Completion of subject delay occurs following *negative* and is realized as *Q* and *subject. Subject* is now completed and is realized as a nominal phrase. If a word auxiliary has not occurred, suffixation of the concord and optional *not* lexemes have not been completed as required by the morphotactics. Thus, one of the following must occur preceding the subject with concord and optional *not:* the first element of *have-en, be-go-ing-to* or *be-ing, be* of the passive verb constitutent *be-en,* linking verb *be* or do_1.

Verb Phrase:

VP / [have-en] [PreV] [be-ing] *(Conj) VP_1

PreV / be-go-ing-to [have-en]

Verb phrase occurs as a single predicate constituent and also as a constituent of an infinite phrase (see above under *Infinitive Phrase*).

The second occurrence of *have-en* (second constituent of *PreV*) presupposes the occurrence of *be-go-ing-to.* No other restriction limits the occurrence of preverb lexemes.

Verb Phrase$_1$:

*(Conj)VP_1 /(VP_2 [NumAdv] [AttP] [PurAdv] [DegAdv]),QuotVP

*(Conj)VP_1 indicates that a verb phrase may be repeated with a conjunction *and, but* or *or.* When a verb phrase is repeated, any lexon that

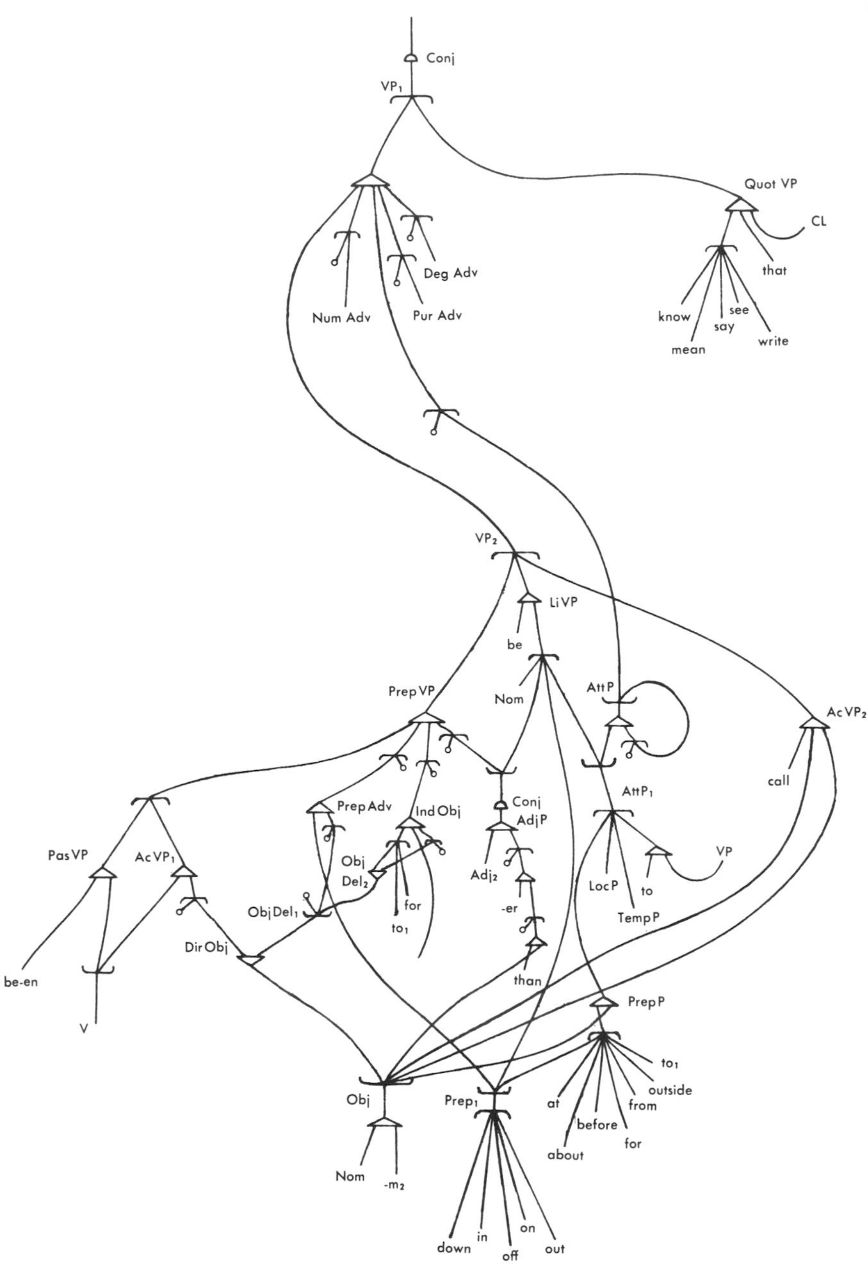
Conj
VP1
Quot VP
CL
that
know
see
say
write
mean
Deg Adv
Num Adv
Pur Adv
VP2
Li VP
be
Prep VP
Nom
Att P
Ac VP2
call
Prep Adv
Ind Obj
Conj
Adj P
Att P1
Pas VP
Ac VP1
Obj
Del2
Adj2
Loc P
to
VP
Obj Del1
for
-er
Temp P
to1
Dir Obj
be-en
than
V
Prep P
to1
outside
at
from
before
for
about
Obj
Prep1
Nom
-m2
on
in
down
off
out

Figure 4

co-occurred with its first occurrence and which the morphotactics specifies as an affix to a verb phrase constituent is also repeated, as though the repetition were the first occurrence of the verb phrase. Thus, in the following sentence the lexon *-ed* is repeated with each successive occurrence of the verb phrase: 'Everyone was scared and jumped up and started running out the door'.

Verb Phrase$_2$:
 VP_2 / PrepVP,LiVP,$AcVP_2$

Verb Phrase$_2$ indicates verb phrases which may be optionally followed by various modifiers: numeral adverb, attributive phrase, purpose adverb and degree adverb. *Quotative verb phrase* does not have modifiers as constituents of the phrase.[3]

Prepositional Verb Phrase:
 PrepVP /(PasVP, $AcVP_1$) [PrepAdv] [IndObj] [*(Conj) CompAdv]

A prepositional verb phrase is characterized by an optional prepositional adverb constituent.

'We have to walk down.'

Passive Verb Phrase:
 PasVP / be-en V
 V / B,have,know,mean,put,write

Base may occur as a verb or a noun (see under *Noun*). A verb may also consist of various lexemes which do not occur as nouns (*have,know,* etc.).

'Everyone was scared.'

Active Verb Phrase$_1$:
 $AcVP_1$ / V [DirObj]
 $AcVP_1$ [ObjDel] / DirObj / Obj

An active verb phrase (*$AcVP_1$, $AcVP_2$*) is characterized by an optional (*$AcVP_1$*) or obligatory (*$AcVP_2$*) occurrence of a direct object.

The second line of an *active verb phrase$_1$* occurring with an optional object delay$_1$ in an upward AND construction is realized as object. This specifies the optional delay of the direct object until following a *preposition$_1$* or an *indirect object,* as described below.

Prepositional Adverb:
 PrepAdv / $Prep_1$ [$ObjDel_1$]
 $Prep_1$ / down,in,off,on,out,up

A *prepositional adverb* may occur following the direct object of an *active verb phrase$_1$* (without an object delay) or preceding the direct object (with an object delay).

'He will write the list out.'
'He will write out the list.'

Indirect Object:

IndObj / $Prep_2$ Obj [$ObjDel_2$]

$Prep_2$ / $ObjDel_2$,to_1,for

$Prep_2$ IndObj / $ObjDel_2$ / $ObjDel_1$

A *preposition*$_2$ may be realized as either the first line of an upward AND (labeled *ObjDel*$_2$), specifying the delay of the direct object until after the indirect object, or as either *to* or *for*. If the impulse of *preposition*$_2$ is *ObjDel*$_2$ it waits for activation of the line following *object. Indirect object* occurs next followed by an impulse to *object delay* which permits the realization of *Obj* which is the direct object of an *active verb phrase*$_1$.

'He will write out me a list.'

The sequence *out me* is adjusted by the morphotactic pattern, which specifies *write me* as a single word. If the third line of *indirect object* is realized as zero, the impulse of *preposition*$_2$ may not pass the upward AND and either *to* or *for* is specified and the direct object is not delayed.

'He will write a list out for me.'

DirObj · (PrepAdv,$ObjDel_2$) / Obj

Comparative Adverb:

*(Conj)CompAdv / (fast, . . .) -er than Obj

'You get down faster.'

Comparative adverb may be repeated with a conjunction:

'You get down faster and safer.'

Linking Verb Phrase:

VPLi / be *(Conj) AdvP,Nom,$Prep_1$,$AttP_1$

AdvP / Adj_2 [CompP]

CompP / -er [than Obj]

For a description of *Adj*$_2$ see above under *Noun Phrase*.

Active Verb Phrase$_2$:

$AcVP_2$ / call Obj Obj

An *active verb phrase*$_2$ consists of *call* (or other verbs not found in the text) followed by two objects. The first is a direct object of the verb, the second a nominative complement. An example of an *active verb phrase*$_2$ occurs in the text involving the relative interrogative pronoun *what*.

'What do you call the other thing?'

Numeral Adverb:

NumAdv / (one,two,three, . . .) -ce

A *numeral adverb* may modify either a *verb phrase*$_2$ or a linking verb phrase:

'I got to hit it once.'

'I was out once.'

Attributive Phrase:

Attributive phrase is described above, where it occurs as the first constituent of a clause.

'I have something to do in that tonight for homework.'

'I was out on first.'

Purpose Adverb:

PurAdv / to-see-if Clause

'They were going to show the pictures to the other schools to see if they would like to have the movie of Harriet Tubman.'

Degree Adverb:

DegAdv / so-much-that Sn

'It scared me so much that I jumped about six feet off the ground.'

Quotative Verb Phrase:

QuotVP / QuotV [that_{3b}] Sn

QuotV / know,mean,say,see,write, . . .

The term "quotative" is used to identify this phrase type and the verbs which are constituents of it, though only a few verbs of this class contain the semantic element of quotation.

'That means that there were three throws.'

Vocative:

Voc / NPers

Personal nouns are described above in the treatment of *nominal.*

'What did you do at school this afternoon, Gordy?'

Exclamatory Sentence:

ExclSn / Excl [com MajSn]

Excl / no [no], oh yea, . . .

'No no!' 'Oh yea!'

Interjection:

Itj / hmh,mhm,m' 'm,nope,u' u', . . .

2.3 Lexicon.

The lexicon is presented in a tabular arrangement of three columns. The first column, labeled *Heading,* for the most part lists lexemes in alphabetical order. A semon with alternate realizations is also listed in this column, thus ^{SN}Fut / will,be-go-ing-to. The lexemes *will* and *be-go-ing-to* are also listed in alphabetical order in this column with a cross-reference in the third column to the semon of which they are realizations. The third column is used only in this situation. The second column, headed *Valence,* indicates the relationship of the lexeme to the lexemic tactic pattern.

HEADING	*VALENCE*	*SEMON*
a	Det	
$about_1$	NumAdj	
$about_2$	Prep	
after-noon	N_1	
all	PrPers	
and	Conj	
any	Det,N_1	
at	Prep	
ball	B	
base	B	
base-ball	N_1	
be	VPLi	
be-en	PasVP	
be-ing	VP	
be-fore	Prep	
be-go-ing-to	PreV	^{SN}Fut
bell	B	
break	B	
but	Conj	
call	B,$AcVP_2$	
can	Aux	
-ce	NumAdv	
chute	N_1	
class	B	
day	N_1	
do	B	
dog	B	
Donello	$NPers_2$	
door	N_1	
down	Prep,$Prep_1$	
draw	B	
else	RIP_2	
-ed	Aux	^{SN}Past
-er	CompAdv	
every-one	PrImp	
fast	Adj_2,CompAdv	
fire-alarm	N_1	
fire-escape	N_1	
first-base	N_1	
foot	B	
for	Prep,$Prep_2$	

HEADING	*VALENCE*	*SEMON*
from	Prep	
^{SN}Fut / will,be-go-ing-to		
get	B	
go	B	
Gordy	$NPers_2$	
great-big	Adj_1	
ground	B	
hang	B	
Harriet	$NPers_2$	
have	V	
have-en	VP,PreV	^{SN}Past
he	PrPers	
help	B	
hit	B	
hmh	Itj	
home-work	N_1	
how-come	MajSn	
I	PrPers	
if	SubClause	
in	Prep,$Prep_1$	
it	PrImp	
jump	B	
just	Pred	
Kathy	$NPers_2$	
know	V,QuotV	
like	B	
$-m_1$	Con	
$-m_2$	Obj	
make	B	
man	B	
mean	V,QuotV	
mhm	Itj	
Mister	NPers	
movie	N_1	
m' 'm	Itj	
no	Excl	
nope	Itj	
not	Pred	
of	PostNMod	
off	Prep,$Prep_1$	
oh	Excl	

HEADING	*VALENCE*	*SEMON*
on	Prep,Prep$_1$	
once	N$_1$	
one	Num,NumAdv	
or	Conj	
other	NP	
-ould	Aux	
out	Prep,Prep$_1$	
out-side$_1$	Prep	
out-side$_2$	LocP	
^{SN}Past / -ed,have-en		
picture	B	
play	B	
put	V	
Q	SubjDel	
-re	Con	
ring	B	
run	B	
run-ing	N$_1$	
-s	Nmb	
-'s	PosNom	
say	B,QuotV	
scare	B	
school	B	
score	B	
second	N$_1$	
see	B,QuotV	
she	PrPers	
show	B	
side	B	
six	Num,NumAdv	
slide	B	
so-much-that	DegAdv	
some	Det	
some-thing	PrImp	
start	B	
step	B	
story	B	
strike	B	
-th	NumOrd	
than	CompAdv	
that$_1$	DemDet	
that$_2$	PrDem	

HEADING	*VALENCE*	*SEMON*
$that_{3a}$	$RelPr_3$	
$that_{3b}$	QuotVP	
the	Det	
then	TempP	
$there_1$	PrImp	
$there_2$	LocP	
they	PrPers	
$this_1$	PrDem	
$this_2$	DemDet	
three	Num,NumAdv	
throw	B	
to_1	Prep,$Prep_2$	
to_2	InfP	
to-day	TempP	
to-night	TempP	
to-see-if	PurAdv	
tube	B	
Tubman	$NPers_2$	
two	Num,NumAdv	
up	Prep,$Prep_1$	
u' 'u	Itj	
walk	B	
we	PrPers	
$what_1$	$RelPr_1$	
$what_2$	IntDet	
$which_1$	$RelPr_3$	
$which_2$	IntDet	
who	$RelPr_2$	
will	Aux	^{SN}Fut
work	B	
write	V,QuotV	
yea	Excl	
yester-day	TempP	
you_1	PrPers	
you_2	PrPers	
$-z_1$	Con	

3. MORPHEMIC SYSTEM

3.1 Morphemic Transcription Of The Text.

The morphemic transcription indicates the occurrence of sequences of morphemes within words. The former are separated by hyphens and the latter by spaces. Portmanteaus are not indicated as such in this transcription, since portmanteau realization is assigned to the morphemic sign pattern, below the morphotactics (see sec. 3.3). Thus *were,* for example, is transcribed *be-re-ed*$_1$.

M: What do$_1$-re-ed$_1$ you do$_2$ at school this after-noon Gordy?
G: Play-ed$_1$ base-ball.
M: Play-ed$_1$ base-ball? Do$_1$-re-ed$_1$ you make any hit-s?
G: No, no.
M: You do$_1$-re-ed$_1$-n't hit it?
G: I get-m$_1$-A$_2$ to hit it one-ce.
F: Do$_1$-re-ed$_1$ you get to one-th base?
G: Nope.
F: How come?
G: I strike-m$_1$-A$_2$ out.
F: Strike-A$_2$ out?
G: Two-th base to one-th and I be-m$_1$-ed$_1$ out.
F: Yea, but you do$_1$-re-ed$_1$-n't strike out then, they put-re-Ø$_2$ you out on one-th.
G: I hit-m$_1$-Ø$_2$ the ball to two-th base, then he throw-Ø$_1$-A$_2$ it to one-th and I be-m$_1$-ed$_1$ out.
F: Yea, if you strike-re out that mean-z$_1$ that there be-re-ed$_1$ three throw-s and you do$_1$-re-ed$_1$-n't hit any of đe-m$_2$.
G: What do$_1$-re you call the other thing?
F: You be-re-ed$_1$ put-Ø$_3$ out on one-th base.
M: What else do$_1$-re-ed$_1$ you do$_2$ in school?
G: We have-re-ed$_1$ Lassie.
M: What-be-z$_1$ that about?
G: About a dog.
M: Yea, but what do$_1$-re-ed$_1$ you have to do.
G: I have-m$_1$ some-thing to do$_2$ in that to-night for home-work.
M: What do$_1$-re-ed$_1$ you do Kathy?
K: Well, we be-re-ed$_1$ write-ing a-s story-s about that Harriet Tubman, and then we draw-re-A$_2$ a-s picture-s, and then he se-Ø$_1$-ed$_1$ they be-re-ed$_1$ go-ing to show the picture-s to other school-s to see if they will-re-ed$_1$ like to have the movie of Harriet Tubman . . . the class of that Mister Donello . . . he-be-z$_1$ the man that be-Ø$_1$-ed$_1$ help-ing the school . . . that show-Ø$_1$-ed$_1$ we-m$_2$ the picture-s, and then the bell ring-Ø$_1$-A$_2$.
F: Hmh?
K: Then the bell ring-Ø$_1$-A$_2$ and we have-re-ed$_1$ to go.
G: To-day we have-re-ed$_1$ a . . . the fire-alarm wen-Ø$_1$-ed$_1$.
K: Oh yea.

G: And it scare-$\emptyset_1$-ed$_1$ I-m$_2$ so much that I jump-m$_1$-ed$_1$ about six foot-A$_1$ off the ground and every-one be-$\emptyset_1$-ed$_1$ scare-ed$_2$ and jump-$\emptyset_1$-ed$_1$ up and start-$\emptyset_1$-ed$_1$ run-ing out the door.
F: Do$_1$-re-ed$_1$ you all go out-side?
G: Mhm.
M: Do$_1$-re-ed$_1$ you go down a chute?
G: Down a fire-escape.
M: Just down the step-s?
G: Mhm.
M: Not a chute huh?
G: U' 'u.
M: A slide? Do$_1$-re they have a slide there?
G: M' 'm.
M: They do$_1$-re-n't have any slide huh? You know-re some school-s have a great big tube and you just slide-re down and you get-re down fast-er.
G: We have-re to walk down.
F: You can-re-ed$_1$-n't run huh?
G: No, we-will-re-ed$_1$ be hang-ed at the break of day.

3.2 Morphemic Tactic Pattern.

The description presented here of the morphemic tactic pattern of words is restricted, for the most part, to combinations of closely-joined units such as bases and affixes. In a few instances, more loosely-joined units are indicated as, for example, the combination of auxiliaries with *not* in the formation of words such as *can't, isn't, didn't,* etc. A development of the morphotactics beyond this preliminary description would include many such groupings, which would give evidence for the various categories distinguished in the formula for *Word* (below). Thus, for example, verb forms listed below under *Verb* would combine with auxiliaries and pronouns (e.g., hiyzgán 'He has gone').

Phrase:
P / W [# P]

A phrase consists of a word followed by optional word juncture and a phrase.

Word:
W / Pr,Subst,Aux,V,Adv,Adj,Det,Prep,W$_s$

Pronoun:
Pr / Pr$_1$,Pr$_2$,ObjPr

Pronoun$_1$:
Pr$_1$ / PosPr [-z$_2$]
PosPr / (aw-,đe-,hɨ-,yɨ-) -r

$Pronoun_1$ is any one of the following: *ours, theirs, hers, yours* or the possessive pronouns *our, their, her* and *your.*

$Pronoun_2$:
Pr_2 / I -'s [-ne]

$Pronoun_2$ is either *my* (portmanteau realization of the two morphemes *I* and *-'s*) or *mine*.

Object Pronoun:
ObjPr / (ðe-,hɨ-,I,she,we,who) $-m_2$

I, she and *we* with $-m_2$ have portmanteau realizations *me, her* and *us.*

Substantive:
Subst / (Pr_s,NPers,NImp,NDet,NumOrd) [-'s]

A substantive may be either a simple pronoun, a personal noun, an impersonal noun or a determiner noun, followed by an optional possessive suffix.

Simple Pronoun:
Pr_s / he,I, it, she,$that_2$,they,$this_1$,we,$which_1$,who,you

Personal Noun:
NPers / Donello,Gordy, Harriet,Kathy,Tubman, . . .

Impersonal Noun:
NImp / $NImp_1$,$NImp_2$

Impersonal $Noun_1$:
$NImp_1$ / (B,N_s,NPrep) [-s]

Base:
B / Num,alarm,ball,base,bell,break,call,class,do_2,dog,draw,escape, fire,foot,get,go,ground,hang,help,hit,home,jump,know,like, make,man,picture,play,put,ring,run,say,scare,school,score,see, show,side,slide,start,step,story,strike,throw,tube,walk,work
Num / one,two, . . .
N_s / chute,day,door,Mister,movie,night,noon,other,they

Prepositional Noun:
NPrep / Prep (B, N_s), before
Prep / at,about,after,down,for,from,in,of,off,on,out,to,up,before
before / be- -fore

The following prepositional nouns occur in the text: *afternoon, today, tonight, outside.* The actual co-occurrence of prepositions and bases is highly restricted and probably the prepositions *from* and *of* do not occur as constituents of prepositional nouns at all. Prosodic patterns vary with different prepositional nouns suggesting the possibility of further subdivisions.

Impersonal Noun$_2$:

NImp$_2$ / (foot,man) [A$_1$]

Impersonal noun$_2$ represents a class of nouns which are pluralized by an ablaut morpheme. The phonemic shape of the vowel of an impersonal noun so pluralized is specified in the phonemic system.

Determiner Nouns:

NDet / Det$_1$ (body,thing)

Det$_1$ / any,every,no,some

Ordinal Numeral:

NumOrd / Num -th

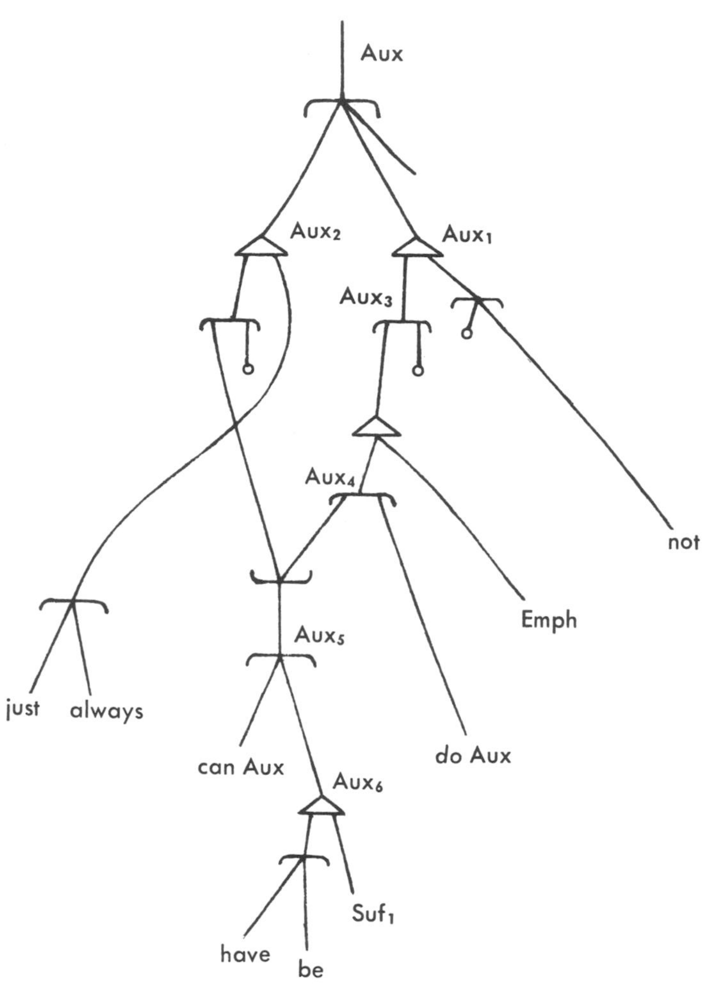

Figure 5

Auxiliary:

Aux / Aux_1,Aux_2,be -en

$Auxiliary_1$ is characterized by an optional constituent *not, $auxiliary_2$* by an adverb constituent *just* or *always.*

$Auxiliary_1$:

Aux_1 /Aux_3 not

$Auxiliary_3$:

Aux_3 / ([Emph] · Aux_4) + Ø

$Auxiliary_3$ specifies an ordered OR, the first line realized at a lower level of the morphotactics as various auxiliaries and the second line realized as zero. This rule requires *not* to be suffixed to an auxiliary if *not* occurs as part of a predicate within the lexemic tactic pattern where auxiliaries may occur. In other environments, *not* occurs as a separate word.

$Auxiliary_4$:

Aux_4 / Aux_5 + *do*Aux

This rule specifies an ordered OR with *do* auxiliary as the second line. The ordering involves two features; the occurrence of auxiliaries with *not* and their occurrence in the formation of question sentences. If *not* is activated and is specified by the lexotactics as a predicate constituent and an *$auxiliary_5$* morpheme is also activated, *not* is suffixed to that auxiliary as specified by the ordering indicated in the above rule.

'You couldn't run, huh?'

However, if an *$auxiliary_5$* morpheme is not activated, then the second line of the ordered OR is chosen and the morphotactic pattern supplies an auxilary *do_1*.

'You didn't hit it?'

The formation of an interrogative sentence involves the activation of the lexeme *Q*. This lexeme is realized in the lexonic alternation pattern as follows: ^{LN}Q / do_1 + Ø. *do_1* is chosen if the morphotactic pattern will permit its occurrence. *$Auxiliary_4$* rule, however, specifies the choice of an *$auxiliary_5$* morpheme if one occurs, in which case ^{LN}Q is realized as zero.

'What's that about?'

If an *$auxiliary_5$* morpheme does not occur, *Q* is realized as *do_1*.

'Did you all go outside?'

do Auxiliary:

*do*Aux / do_1 Suf_1

Suf_1 / Con_1,Suf_2

Con_1 / -m_1,-re,-z_1

Suf_2 / Con_2 -ed_1

Con_2 / -m_1,-re,$Ø_1$

-m_1 and *-re* when affixed to *do_1* are realized as zero as specified by the morphemic sign pattern (3.3.1). The phonemic shape of the special vowel

morphon of *do* with the various suffixes described here (*do, does, did*) is specified in the phonemic system.

Auxiliary$_5$:

Aux$_5$ / *can*Aux,Aux$_6$

Auxiliary$_6$ consists of any of the inflected forms of *be* and *have*$_1$. *Auxiliary*$_6$ may be inflected by the third singular concord morpheme -z_1 (*has, is*) whereas a *can* auxiliary (*can, will,* etc.) may only be inflected by the third singular concord morpheme $\emptyset_1$.

can Auxiliary:

*can*Aux / (can,will) Suf$_3$

Suf$_3$ / Con$_2$ [-ed$_1$][4]

The phonemic shape of *can* and *will* with the past morpheme -*ed*$_1$ is specified by the phonemic system.

Auxiliary$_6$:

Aux$_6$ / (have$_1$,be) [Suf$_1$]

For a description of *Suf*$_1$, see above under *do Auxiliary.*

Auxiliary$_2$:

Aux$_2$ / (Aux$_5$ + $\emptyset$) just

Auxiliary$_2$ has, as one constituent, an *auxiliary*$_5$ or a zero in an ordered OR. This rule requires *just* to be suffixed to an *auxiliary*$_5$ (various inflected forms of *can, will, be* or *have*) if *just* is activated as part of a predicate within the lexemic tactic pattern and if an *auxiliary*$_5$ is also activated. If an *auxiliary*$_5$ is not activated, the first constituent of *auxiliary*$_2$ is realized as zero.

'I just ran down the steps.'

Verb:

V / V$_s$ Con$_1$,PastV Con$_2$,PastPartV, PresPartV

A verb is either a simple verb and a *concord*$_1$ morpheme, a past tense verb and a *concord*$_2$ morpheme, a verb inflected with a past participle morpheme or a verb inflected with a present participle morpheme.

For a description of *concord*$_1$ and *concord*$_2$ see above under *do Auxiliary.*

Simple Verb:

V$_s$ / B,come,have$_2$,mean,write

Base (*B*) is described above under *Impersonal Noun.*

Past Verb:

PastV / PastV$_1$,PastV$_2$,PastV$_3$,PastV$_4$

PastV$_1$ / V$_1$ A$_2$

V$_1$ / break,come,draw,get,hang,know,ring,run,see,slide,strike,throw, write

A_2 is a past tense ablaut morpheme. The phonemic shape of the vowels of V_1 with *$ablaut_2$* is specified in the phonemic system.

PastV$_2$ / (mean,say) A-ed

Mean and *say* occur with a past tense morpheme of two constituents. The first is an ablaut and the second a suffix *-d*. Adjustment of the final consonant of *meant* is made within the phonemic system.

PastV$_3$ / (hit,put) $\emptyset_2$

Past tense morpheme with *hit* and *put* is realized as zero within the morphemic knot pattern.

PastV$_4$ / V$_s$ -ed$_1$

The phonemic shape of the following is specified below the morphemic knot pattern: the special final consonant morphon of *have* with *-ed*$_1$ (and with the various concord morphemes); the final consonant morphon of *make* with *-ed*$_1$; the final consonant morphon of *went.*

Past Participle Verb:

PastPartV / PastPart$_1$,PastPart$_2$,PastPart$_3$,PastPart$_4$,PastPart$_5$
PastPartV$_1$ / V$_2$ A$_3$
V$_2$ / hang,ring,slide,strike

The phonemic shape of the vowels of V_2 with *$ablaut_3$* is specified in the phonemic stystem.

PastPartV$_2$ / V$_3$ A-en
V$_3$ / break,get,go,write
PastPartV$_3$ / V$_4$ -en
V$_4$ / draw,know,see,show,throw
PastPartV$_4$ / (hit,put,run) $\emptyset_3$
PastPartV$_5$ / B -ed$_2$

Present Participle:

PresPart / V$_s$ -ing

Adverb:

Adv / Adv$_1$,all,how,there$_1$,then,what$_1$,when

Adv$_1$ / (one,twi-, thri-) -ce

All adverbs occur with contractions of *be, will,* etc. as single morphological words, e.g., *all's* 'all is', *how'd* 'how would', etc.

Adjective:

Adj / AdjComp,Adj$_s$

Comparative Adjective:

AdjComp / Adj$_s$ (-er,-st)

Simple Adjective:

Adj$_s$ / big,fast,great, . . .

Determiner:

Det / Det_1,Det_2

For a description of *determiner*$_1$ see above under *Determiner Nouns.*

Det_2 / (a,$that_1$,$this_2$) [-s]

The determiners *a, that*$_1$ and *this*$_2$ occur with an optional plural morpheme *-s.* *a* with plural is realized in the morphemic sign pattern as zero, and the latter two determiners with plural are realized as portmanteaus *those* and *these.* The determiner lexemes *any, the, some, what*$_2$ and *which*$_2$ are specified by the lexotactic pattern as optionally occurring with *-s.* The morphotactic pattern, however, does not combine these determiners with *-s;* it thus forces the choice of Ø (second line of an ordered OR) as the realization of *-s* within the lexonic alternation pattern.

Simple Word:

W_s / a,and,but,else,if,mhm,m' 'm,nope,oh,or,so,$that_3$,the, $there_2$, u' 'u, well,$what_2$,which,yea,yes, . . .

that$_3$ represents the lexemes *that*$_{3a}$ and *that*$_{3b}$.

3.3 Morphemic Sign Pattern (upper portion).

The lower portion of the morphemic sign pattern (i.e., from morphemic signs to morphons) is not included in this description.

3.3.1. *Zero Realization.*

$-m_1$ / (am,was) + Ø

-m$_1$ combines with *be* to realize portmanteaus *am* or *was* (see below); otherwise *-m*$_1$ is realized as zero.

-re / (are,were) + Ø

$-z_1$ / is + Ø

$-Ø_1$ / was + Ø

3.3.2 *Portmanteaus.*

Pronoun:

I -'s /my

I $-m_2$ /me

she $-m_2$ /her

we $-m_2$ /us

Linking Verb:

be $-m_1$ /am

be $-m_1$ $-ed_1$ /was

be -re /are

be -re $-ed_1$ /were

be $-z_1$ /is

be $Ø_1$ $-ed_1$ /was

Noun Suffixes:

-s -'s /s

'the boys' ball'

Determiner:

a -s /Ø
this -s /these
that -s /those

Ordinal Numerals:

one -th /first
two -th /second
three -th /third

3.4 Morphicon.

The morphicon, like the lexicon, is presented in a tabular arrangement of three columns. The first column, labeled *Heading* includes an alphabetical arrangement of symbols for morphemes and lexons, including lexons with diversification. Lexons realized as single morphemes are not separately indicated. The second column indicates the relationship of the morphemes to the morphotactic pattern. The third column, labeled *Lexon,* indicates the lexon when the morpheme of the first column is one of two or more realizations. The realization of some lexons includes a zero (Ø) in an ordered OR (e.g., ^{LN}Q / do_1 + Ø). This specifies that the lexon is realized as zero if the morphotactic pattern so requires. A numbered zero (e.g., $Ø_1$) indicates a morpheme which is realized as zero in the knot pattern. The specification "(ordered AND)" indicates that the upward AND of the knot pattern is ordered (with the line from the tactics second).

HEADING	*VALENCE*	*LEXON*
a	Det_2	
A_1	$NImp_2$	^{LN}-s
A_2	$PastV_1$ (ordered AND)	^{LN}-ed
A_3	$PastPartV^1$ (ordered AND)	^{LN}-en
about	Prep	
A- ed	$PastV_2$ (ordered AND)	^{LN}-ed
A-en	$PastPartV_2$ (ordered AND)	^{LN}-en
after	Prep	
alarm	B	
all	Adv	
and	W_s	
any	Det	
at	Prep	
aw-	PosPr	^{LN}we
ball	B	
base	B	
be	Aux,Aux_6	

HEADING	*VALENCE*	*LEXON*
be-	before	
bell	B	
big	Adj_s	
body	NDet	
break	B,V_1,V_3	
but	W_s	
call	B	
can	*can*Aux	
-ce	Adv_1	
chute	N_s	
class	B	
come	V_1,V_s	
day	N_s	
de-	PosPr,ObjPr	^{LN}they
do_1	*do*Aux	^{LN}Q
do_2	B	
dog	B	
Donello	NPers	
door	N_s	
down	Prep	
draw	B,V_1,V_4	
^{LN}-ed / (A_2, A-ed, Ø) + $-ed_1$		
$-ed_1$	$Suf_2,Suf_3,PastV_4$	^{LN}-ed
$-ed_2$	$PastPartV_5$ (ordered AND)	^{LN}-en
else	W_s	
^{LN}-en / A_3,A-en,-en, / $Ø_3$,$-ed_2$		
-en	Aux,$PastPartV_3$	^{LN}-en
-er	AdjComp	
escape	B	
every	Det	
fast	Adj_s	
fire	B	
foot	B,$NImp_2$	
for	Prep	
-fore	before	
from	Prep	
get	B,V_1,V_3	
go	B,V_3	
Gordy	NPers	
great	Adj_s	

HEADING	*VALENCE*	*LEXON*
ground	B	
hang	B,V_1,V_2	
Harriet	NPers	
$have_1$	Aux_6	
$have_2$	V_s	
LNhe / hɨ-,he		
he	Pr_s	LNhe
help	B	
hi-	ObjPr	LNhe
hɨ-	PosPr	LNshe
hit	B,PastV_3,PastPartV_4	
home	B	
how	Adv	
I	Pr_2,ObjPr,Pr_s	
if	W_s	
in	Prep	
-ing	PresPart (ordered AND)	
it	Pr_s	
jump	B	
just	Aux_2	
Kathy	NPers	
know	B,V_1,V_4	
like	B	
-m_1	Con_1,Con_2 (ordered AND)	
LN-m_2 / $m_2 + \emptyset$		
-m_2	ObjPr	LN-m_2
make	B	
man	B,$NImp_2$	
mean	V_s,PastV_2	
mhm	W_s	
Mister	N_s	
movie	N_s	
m' 'm	W_s	
-ne	Pr_2	
night	N_s	
no	Det	
noon	N_s	
nope	W_s	
not	Aux_1	
of	Prep	
off	Prep	
oh	W_s	

HEADING	*VALENCE*	*LEXON*
on	Prep	
one	Num,Adv_1	
or	W_s	
other	N_s	
out	Prep	
picture	B	
play	B	
put	B,$PastV_3$,$PastPartV_4$	
^{LN}Q / do_1 + Ø		
-r	PosPr	^{LN}- s
-re	Con_1,Con_2 (ordered AND)	
ring	B,V_1,V_2	
run	B,V_1,$PastPartV_4$	
^{LN} / A_1,-s + Ø		
-s	$NImp_1$,Det_2	^{LN}-s
^{LN}-'s / -r,-'s		
-'s	Pr_2,Subst	^{LN}-'s
say	B,$PastV_2$	
scare	B	
school	B	
score	B	
see	B,V_1,V_4	
^{LN}she / hɨ,she		
she	ObjPr,Pr_S	^{LN}she
show	B,V_4	
side	B	
six	Num	
slide	B,V_1,V_2	
so	W_s	
some	Det	
-st	AdjComp	
start	B	
step	B	
story	B	
strike	B,V_1,V_2	
-th	NumOrd	
$that_1$	Det_2	
$that_2$	Pr_s	
$that_3$	W_s	
the	W_s	
then	Adv_2	
$there_1$	Adv	

HEADING	*VALENCE*	*LEXON*
there_2	W_s	
^{LN}they / đe-,they		
they	Pr_s	^{LN}they
thing	N_s,NDet	
this_1	Pr_s	
this_2	Det_2	
^{LN}three / thri-,three		
three	Num	^{LN}three
thri-	Adv_1	^{LN}three
throw	B,V_1,V_4	
to	Prep	
tube	B	
Tubman	NPers	
twi-	Adv_1	^{LN}two
^{LN}two / twi-,two		
two	Num	^{LN}two
up	Prep	
u' 'u	W_s	
walk	B	
^{LN}we / aw-,we		
we	ObjPr,Pr_s	^{LN}we
well	W_s	
what_1	Adv	
what_2	W_s	
when	Adv	
which_1	Pr_s	
which_2	W_s	
who	ObjPr,Pr_s	
will	*can*Aux	
work	B	
write	V_s,V_1,V_3	
yea	W_s	
yes	W_s	
yɨ-	PosPr	^{LN}you
^{LN}you / yɨ-,you		
you	Pr_s	^{LN}you
^{LN}-z_1 / $\emptyset_1$,z_1		
-z_1	Con_1 (ordered AND)	^{LN}-z_1
-z_2	PosPr	
$\emptyset_1$	Con_2	^{LN}-z_1
$\emptyset_2$	$PastV_4$ (ordered AND)	^{LN}-ed
$\emptyset_3$	$PastPartV_4$ (ordered AND)	^{LN}-en

ABBREVIATIONS

Ac	active
Adj	adjective
Adv	adverb
Att	attributive
Aux	auxiliary
B	base
com	comma
Comp	comparative
Con	concord
Conj	conjunction
D, Det	determiner
Deg	degree
Del	delay
Dem	demonstrative
Dir	direct
Emph	emphasis
Excl	exclamatory
Imp	impersonal
Ind	indirect
Inf	infinitive
Int	interrogative
Itj	interjection
Li	linking
Loc	locative
Maj	major
Mod	modifier
N	noun
Nom	nominal
Nuc	nucleus
Num	numeral
Nmb	number
Obj	object
Ord	ordinal
P	phrase
Part	participle
Pas	passive
Past	past
Pers	personal
Pos	possessive
Post	post
Pr	pronoun
PreV	preverb

Pres	present
Pred	predicate
Prep	preposition
Pur	purpose
Quot	quotative
Rel	relative
RIP	relative interrogative pronoun
Sn	sentence
s	simple
Sub	subordinate
Subj	subject
Subst	substantive
Suf	suffix
Temp	temporal
V	verb
Voc	vocative
W	word

Footnotes:

[1] In all sections of this description I am indebted to Sydney Lamb for suggested analyses, obtained from his writings, published and mimeographed materials, classroom lectures and from oral discussions with him regarding particular problems as they have arisen. His help has been so extensive that only a general acknowledgement is possible here. Acknowledgement is also made to David Bennett who drew the graphs for this supplement.

[2] Conventional orthography is used in symbolizing most lexemes and morphemes. Phonemic transcription is used only when conventional transcription is not useful in identifying the unit, (e.g., *đe-* 'third plural pronoun').

[3] A quotative verb phrase, however, has a clause as one of its constituents which may contain one of these modifiers: 'He said that the fire alarm went today at school'.

[4] The lexemes *-ould* and *-ed* are neutralized and are realized as the lexon *-ed*.

INDEX